KU-241-977

Saffy's Angel

QF MCK Teen fiction
152014

Saffy's Angel

Hilary McKay

Winner of the 2002 Whitbread Children's Award

HODDER LITERATURE

www.hodderliterature.co.uk

Other titles in the Hodder Literature series:

The Fire-Eaters by David Almond
(ISBN 0 340 88349 9)

Kit's Wilderness by David Almond
(ISBN 0 340 88350 2)

Secret Heart by David Almond
(ISBN 0 340 88351 0)

Skellig by David Almond
(ISBN 0 340 90554 9)

Skellig: The Play by David Almond
(ISBN 0 340 90555 7)

Control-Shift by Nick Manns
(ISBN 0 340 89986 7)

Stratford Boys by Jan Mark
(ISBN 0 340 88354 5)

Mondays are Red by Nicola Morgan
(ISBN 0 340 88353 7)

Shadow of the Beast by Maggie Pearson
(ISBN 0 340 89988 3)

Bad Alice: In the Shadow of the Red Queen by Jean Ure
(ISBN 0 340 88357 X)

To order **Saffy's Angel** or any of the other books
in the Hodder Literature series, please contact
Bookpoint on 01235 827720.

To Kevin

Chapter One

When Saffron was eight, and had at last learned to read, she hunted slowly through the colour chart pinned up on the kitchen wall.

It was a painter's colour chart, from an artists' materials shop. It showed all the colours a painter could ever need. There were rows and rows of little squares, each a different shade of red or blue or green or golden yellow. Every little square had the name of the colour underneath. To the Casson children those names were as familiar as nursery rhymes. Other families had lullabies, but the Cassons had fallen asleep to lists of colours.

Saffron found Indigo almost at once, a smoky dark blue on the bottom row of the chart. Indigo was two years younger than Saffron. His name suited him exactly.

'If there is one thing your mother was good at,' Bill Casson, the children's father would say, 'it was choosing names for you children!'

Eve, the children's mother, would always look pleased. She never protested that there might be more than one thing that she was good at, because she never thought there was.

Indigo was a thin, dark-haired little boy with anxious indigo-coloured eyes. He had a list in his head of things that did not matter (such as school), and another list of things that did. High on Indigo's list of things that mattered was his pack. That was how he thought of his sisters. His pack.

Saffron was the middle one of the pack.

Saffron had to climb on to a stool to see the colour chart properly. The stool had a top of woven string that was coming unwoven, and its legs rocked on the irregular tiles of the kitchen floor.

'I can't find me,' she grumbled to Indigo, wobbling on the stool. 'I can't find Saffron written anywhere.'

'What about the rest of us?' asked Indigo, not looking up. 'What about the baby?'

Indigo was crouched on the hearth rug sorting through the coal bucket. Pieces of coal lay all around. Sometimes he found lumps speckled with what he believed to be gold. He looked like a small black devil in the shadowy room with the firelight behind him.

'Come and help me look for Saffron!' pleaded Saffron.

'Find the baby first,' said Indigo.

Indigo did not like the baby to be left out of anything that was going on. This was because for a long time after she was born it had seemed she would be left out of everything, and for ever. She had very nearly eluded his pack. She had very nearly died. Now she was safe and easy to find, third row up at the end of the pinks. Rose. Permanent Rose.

2

Rose was screaming because the health visitor had arrived to look at her. She had turned up unexpectedly, from beyond the black, rainy windows and picked up Rose with her strong, cold hands, and so Rose was screaming.

'Make Rose shut up!' shouted Saffron from her stool. 'I'm trying to read!'

'Saffron reads anything now!' the children's mother told the health visitor proudly.

'Very nice!' the health visitor replied, and Saffron looked pleased for a moment, but then stopped when the health visitor added that her twins had both been fluent readers at four years old, and had gone right through their junior school library by the age of six.

Saffron glanced across to Caddy, the eldest of the Casson children, to see if this could possibly be true. Caddy, aged thirteen, was absorbed in painting the soles of her hamster's feet, but she felt Saffron's unhappiness and gave her a quick, comforting smile. Since Rose's arrival the Casson family had heard an awful lot about the health visitor's multi-talented twins. They were in Caddy's class at school. There were a number of rude and true things that Caddy might have said about them, but being Caddy, she kept them to herself. Her smile was enough.

Caddy appeared over and over on the colour chart, all along the top row. Cadmium Lemon, Cadmium Deep Yellow, Cadmium Scarlet and Cadmium Gold.

No Saffron though.

'There *isn't* a Saffron,' said Saffron after another long

search. 'I've looked, and there isn't! I've read it all, and there *isn't*!'

Nobody seemed to hear at first. Caddy continued painting her hamster's feet. The baby continued screaming. Eve continued explaining to the health visitor (who frightened her very much) that she had not noticed anything at all wrong with Rose until the health visitor had pointed it out, and the health visitor continued tut-tutting.

'*I can't find Saffron!*' complained Saffron crossly.

Indigo said, 'Saffron's yellow.'

'I *know* Saffron's yellow!'

'Well then, look under the yellows,' said Indigo, and tipped the whole of the coal bucket upside down in the hearth, enveloping his end of the room in a cloud of coal dust.

This made the health visitor start coughing as well as tutting.

'I don't know how you keep your patience!' she said to Eve. Her voice showed that she thought it would be much better if Eve did not. She had dropped in to weigh Rose, as she often did, and had noticed at once that the baby had gone a very strange colour. A sort of brownish mustard. She seemed to think it was a terrible thing that Rose should have gone mustard without anybody noticing. She began undressing her.

'I've looked under *all* the yellows,' said Saffron loudly and belligerently, 'and I've looked under *all* the oranges too, and there *isn't* a Saffron!'

Rose wailed even louder because she didn't want to be undressed. Her mother said, 'Oh, darling! Darling!' Indigo began hammering at likely-looking lumps of coal with the handle end of the poker. Caddy let the hamster walk across the table and it made a delicate and beautiful pattern of rainbow-coloured footprints all over the health visitor's notes.

'*Why* isn't there a Saffron?' demanded Saffron. 'There's all the others. What about me?'

Then the health visitor said the thing that changed Saffron's life. She looked up from unpicking something out of Rose's clenched fist and said to the children's mother:

'Doesn't Saffron know?'

The words fell into a moment of silence. Rose held her breath between roars. Caddy's head jerked up and her eyes were startled. Indigo stopped hammering. Eve went scarlet and looked very confused and began an unhappy mumble. A not-yet, not-now sort of mumble.

'Know what?' asked Saffron, looking from the health visitor to her mother.

'Nothing, dear,' said the health visitor in a bright, careless voice, and Saffron, who had been frightened without knowing why, allowed herself to believe this was true.

'Nothing, nothing!' repeated the health visitor, half singing the words, and then in a completely different voice, 'Good heavens! What on earth is this?'

Rose's fist had come undone, revealing that she held

a tube of paint (Yellow Ochre), obviously very much sucked.

'Paint!' said the health visitor, absolutely horrified. '*Paint*! PAINT! She's had a tube of paint! This household ... I don't know! *She's been sucking a tube of paint!*'

'What colour?' asked Indigo immediately.

'Yellow Ochre,' Caddy told him. 'I gave it to her. I didn't think she'd suck it. Anyway, I'm only using non-toxic colours.'

'Caddy!' said her mother, laughing. 'No wonder she's gone such a funny colour!'

'I'm ringing the hospital!' said the health visitor, in a voice of controlled calm. 'Wrap her up in something warm! Don't give her anything to drink! We'll go straight to Casualty ...'

Then for a while Saffron forgot her worries while they all tried to convince the health visitor that none of Caddy's colours were in the least poisonous, and that Rose, except for needing washing, was quite all right.

'But *why* did you give it to her?' the health visitor asked Caddy.

'To make her let go of the Chinese White,' said Caddy.

'Chinese White's sweet,' explained Saffron, and then there was another fuss. While it was going on Indigo got bored and went back to his gold hunting, bashing a lump of coal so hard that pieces flew everywhere, and the baby got a chunk to suck, and the hamster jumped in fright into the health visitor's bag, and the health visitor said, 'Thank goodness my twins! . . . If that hamster has made a mess . . . I suppose this is what they call artistic . . .'

'Yes,' said Eve eagerly. 'They are all very . . .'

'You need the patience of a saint in my job!' said the health visitor as she left.

After she had gone the children's mother hunted through the kitchen cupboards looking for something for tea. While she was doing it she cried a bit because it was so hard being an artist with four children to look after, especially in wet weather when rain blew under the kitchen door and down all the chimneys and into the bonnet of the car so that it would not start and she could not get to the supermarket. She thought wistfully of the shed at the end of the garden, her favourite place in the world.

Only Rose noticed she was crying. Rose watched her with unsurprised blue eyes, enjoying the sniffs.

The kitchen cupboard was full of non-food sorts of food. Lentils and cereal and packet sauces and jam. Eve had almost given up hope when she unearthed a large and completely unexpected tin of baked beans, the sort with sausages in, a small miracle.

'Daddy must have bought them!' she exclaimed, as happy as she had been miserable a moment before.

The beans changed everything. Saffron took over the toaster. Caddy put the hamster into its cage and cleared the table. Indigo picked up his lumps of coal. Permanent

Rose sucked a crust of bread and smiled at everyone and waited patiently until someone should think of scrambling her an egg. Eve stirred the beans and sausages and was grateful to Bill Casson, the children's father. He was a real artist, not a garden shed one like herself. He was such a very real artist that he could only work in London. He rented a small studio at enormous expense, and only came home at weekends. Real artists, he often explained to Caddy and Saffron and Indigo, cannot work with three children under their feet and a baby that wakes up several times every night.

'Clever, clever Daddy, buying beans!' said Eve.

'Rose could have an egg,' suggested Caddy, reading Rose's mind.

'I wonder if Dad bought anything else,' said Indigo, and he and Saffron at once began searching the kitchen cupboards themselves, hoping for more surprises. A lump of coal turned up, with a glitter of gold on it, and a bag of squashed pink and white marshmallows which they floated on hot chocolate and shared with Rose from the end of a spoon.

It was a very happy evening and bedtime before Saffron asked again, 'Why isn't my name on the colour chart? Why isn't there a Saffron?'

'Saffron is a lovely colour,' said her mother evasively.

'But it's not on the chart.'

'Well . . .'

'The others are.'

'Yes.'

'But not me.'

8

'I thought of calling you Siena. Or Scarlet.'

'Why didn't you?'

There was a long, long pause.

'It wasn't me who chose your name.'

'Dad?'

'No. Not Daddy. My sister.'

'Your sister who died?'

'Yes. Go to sleep, Saffy. Rose is crying. I've got to go.'

'Siena,' whispered Saffy.

Saffy had a dream that came over and over. In the dream was a white paved place with walls. A sunny place, quiet and enclosed. There were little dark pointed trees and there was the sound of water. The blue sky was too bright to look at. In the dream something was lost. In the dream Saffy cried. In the dream was the word, Siena.

Caddy's bed was close enough to touch. Saffy could tell by the feel of the darkness that she was awake.

She said, 'Caddy, how long ago can you remember?'

'Oh,' said Caddy, 'ages. I can remember when I could only lie flat. On my back. I can remember how pleased I was when I learned to roll.'

'You can't!'

'I can. And I remember learning to crawl. It hurt my knees.'

'No one can remember that far back!'

'Well, I can. I remember it quite clearly. The burny feeling it gave my knees.'

'Do you remember a white stone garden?'

'What white stone garden?'

'Siena.'

'No,' said Caddy. 'That was you, not me.'

The next morning Indigo gave Saffron his gold-speckled lump of coal, and Cadmium added an extra colour square to the top row of the paint chart, Saffron Yellow. In London Bill Casson shut up his small (and very expensive) studio midweek, and caught the first train home.

None of these things meant anything at all to Saffron. All she could think of was the terrible news that she had forced from Eve the night before. Bit by bit, while Rose slept and Indigo argued and Caddy watched and was silent, Saffron had dragged it out.

That was how she discovered that Eve was not her mother. Nor was a real (and nearly successful) artist in London her father. Worst of all, Caddy and Indigo and Rose were not her brother and sisters.

'You're not my family,' said Saffron.

'We are!' cried Eve. 'Of course we are! We adopted you! We wanted you! Your mother was my sister! Caddy and Indigo and Rose are your cousins!'

'That doesn't count,' said Saffron.

'I'm not doing this right,' said Eve, weeping. 'There are books on how to do it right. I have read them. You were only three. You looked just like Caddy. You called me Mummy. You were so happy. Almost as soon as you arrived, you were happy!'

'Why was it a secret?'

'It wasn't a secret!' protested Eve, trying to hug Saffron (who ducked). 'I was waiting for the right time to tell you, that's all. And the longer I left it, the harder it was. I should have done right from the start!'

'Caddy knew! And didn't tell me!'

'I forgot,' said Caddy.

'Forgot!'

'Nearly always.'

'No wonder I'm not on the colour chart,' said Saffron.

Everything seemed to change for Saffron after the day she deciphered the colour chart, and discovered that her name was not there, and found out why this was. She never felt the same again. She felt lost.

'But everything *is* just the same,' said Bill, trying to help. 'Nothing has changed, Saffy darling. We love you just as much as we ever did. You are just as much ours as you always were.'

'No I'm not,' said Saffy.

Eve produced photographs of Saffy's mother, but they were very confusing. Saffron's mother had been Eve's twin sister. They were so alike that even Eve had to puzzle over some of the pictures before she could say who was who.

'What about my father?' Saffron asked.

This was a difficult question. Saffron's mother had never told Eve anything about Saffron's father.

'Your mummy never talked about him,' she said at last.

'Not even to you?'

'Well,' said Eve, sighing as she remembered. 'She was in Italy and I was in England. So it was difficult. I was always going to go and visit her, and I never quite did. I wish I had.'

'Was she an artist? Like you.'

'Oh no,' said Eve. 'Linda was much cleverer than me! She taught English. In Italy. In Siena. You were born in Siena, that's why I thought it would make such a good name . . .'

Saffron was not listening. She looked at the picture of her mother again and said, 'Anyway she's dead.'

'Yes.'

'Killed in a car crash.'

'Yes, darling.'

'Where was I? Did I see her dead?'

'No,' said Eve with relief. 'You were at home. At your home in Siena. With Grandad. He was visiting.'

'Grandad!'

'Yes. He was there when it happened. He brought you back here to us.'

'Grandad did?'

'Yes, Grandad did. He wasn't always like he is now, Saffy darling.'

The Cassons' grandfather was like nothing at all. He lived in a nursing home. He sat. Sometimes in summer he sat in the garden, guided there with a nurse at each side. Sometimes he sat in a lounge and looked at a television which was not always switched on. Often

Eve would collect him and bring him back home with her and he would sit there instead.

Only once, in all his years of sitting had he said a word to show that he remembered anything at all of his previous life. He had said, 'Saffron.'

Everyone had heard.

'Is Grandad still my grandad?' Saffron asked Eve, when it seemed that the whole pattern of her family was slipping and changing, like colours in water, into something she hardly recognised.

Eve said that of course he was. Just as he had always been. Exactly the same.

'But was he my grandad right from the *beginning*?' persisted Saffron, determined to have the truth this time. 'Like he was Caddy's and Indigo's and Rose's?'

'Yes,' said Eve at once, and Caddy added,

'He is *just* as much your grandad as ours, Saffy. More.'

'More?' asked Saffron suspiciously.

'Much more,' said Caddy, 'because he remembers you. He knows your name. Everybody heard. He said "Saffron".'

'Yes he did,' agreed Saffron, and allowed herself to feel a tiny bit comforted.

Caddy was the only one of the Casson children who could recall the days when their grandfather could drive and walk and talk and do things like anybody else. She told Saffron about the evening when he had arrived at the house, bringing Saffron home.

'He had a green car. A big green car and it was full of toys. He'd brought all your toys, he told us. Every crayon. Every scrap of paper. You used to pick up stones, he said. Little bits of stone. He brought them all. In a tin.'

Nothing was ever thrown away in the Casson family. Saffron went upstairs to the bedroom she shared with Caddy and Rose and raked around until she found the scratched blue coffee tin. The stones were still there, bits of gold sandstone, marble chips and a fragment of a red roof tile.

'Grandad said, "She's cried all the way. Not for her mother. For something else. I should have managed to bring it somehow. I promised I would. I shall have to go back."'

'What was he talking about?'

'I don't know. He went away, that same night. We didn't see him again for ages and ages and when we did he was different.'

'What sort of different?'

'Like he is now,' said Caddy.

Chapter Two

The Casson house had been chosen by the children's parents before Caddy was born. They had liked it because it was unspoilt. Unspoilt meant no central heating, coal fires in every room (even the bedrooms and kitchen), and its own particular smell which was a mixture of dampness and soot and a sort of green smell that came in from the garden. The garden always seemed to be trying to sneak its way into the house. Ivy crept in through the cracks around the window panes. Woodlice and beetles and ants and snails had their own private entrances. In autumn dead leaves swirled in every time a door was opened, and in spring live birds fell down the chimneys.

The house had a name. The Banana House. It was carved on to a piece of sandstone above the front door. It made no sense to anyone.

It stood in the middle of a long road. At one end of the road were smart houses with gravelled drives, but the Banana House was not one of those. At the other end were little cottages with bright new paint and tidy gardens. The Banana House was not one of those either. It was quite alone in the middle.

'A disgrace to both ends!' Bill Casson thought once, on one of his brief visits from London, and he wondered why it never occurred to Eve that she might paint the windows and tidy the overgrown grass and grow flowers in the garden. The only things that grew in the garden were guinea pigs. Caddy owned at least half a dozen of them, scattered around in ramshackle runs and hutches. Occasionally they escaped and flocked and multiplied over the lawn like wildebeest on the African plains. Like the hamsters in the house, the guinea pigs on the lawn were Caddy's responsibility. Only she was really interested in them. Caddy, and a child in a wheelchair from one of the smart houses up the road.

Time passed, but the Banana House stayed the same. Generations of guinea pigs came and went. Years went by so quickly that Bill and Eve constantly lost track of the children's ages. Caddy and Saffron grew long legs and long gold hair. Indigo took to dressing entirely in black. Rose started school.

'At last,' said the health visitor, disapprovingly. 'She ought to have gone a year ago!'

'She was so delicate,' pleaded Eve.

'Not any more,' said the health visitor. 'She is quite robust now! *Very* robust, in fact!'

Eve looked so shocked at this opinion that Rose asked Saffron privately, 'What does robust mean?'

'Tough,' said Saffron.

Rose looked pleased.

★ ★ ★

Rose drew a picture of the Banana House on her first day at school that made it look exactly like a banana with windows.

In Rose's picture the garden streamed from the roof of the house like a banner in the wind, bright green and covered in giant guinea pigs. At the end of the garden was a rainbow-coloured box.

'Mummy's shed,' explained Rose, and drew her mother on the roof.

'What is she doing?' asked the teacher.

'Waving,' said Rose.

There were people waving out of the windows too. Rose coloured them in as well as she could with horrible school wax crayons.

'Caddy, Saffron, Indigo and me,' she said. 'Waving goodbye.'

'Who to?'

'Daddy,' said Rose.

Waving goodbye to Daddy was as much a part of Casson life as the colour chart on the kitchen wall, and the guinea pigs on the grass, and the girl in the wheelchair.

Once Rose had pointed to her.

'Don't point!' her father had snapped furiously. '*Don't* point and *don't* stare!'

None of the Cassons pointed or stared, but the wheelchair girl still kept going past the house now and then. She remained a stranger. Rose did not put her into the picture of the banana-shaped house.

Rose's work of art took her all day, including two playtimes, storytime and most of lunch.

At the end of school it was stolen from her by the wicked teacher who had pretended to be so interested.

'Beautiful–what–is–it?' she asked, as she pinned it high on the wall, where Rose could not reach.

'They take your pictures,' said Indigo, who was waiting for Rose at the school gate, when he finally made out what all the roaring and stamping was about. 'They do take them. You have to not care.'

Indigo was now eleven, in the top class of the Primary School, the opposite end to Rose. He was still small and thin, but less anxious now. He had learned to write his problems down in lists and this made him feel more in control. He still thought of his sisters as his pack.

'Why do you want that picture so much?' he asked Rose.

'It was my best ever,' said Rose, furiously. 'I hate school. I hate everyone in it. I will kill them all when I'm big enough.'

'You can't just go round killing people,' Indigo told her, but he looked at her hunched-up shoulders and her drooping head, and thought it was sad to see Rose, Permanent Rose, usually such a cheerful and obstinate member of his pack, completely changed after one day at school.

'Sometimes they give them back at the end of term,' he told her comfortingly. 'Anyway, you can always do another. Let's go home!'

'It was my best *ever*,' repeated Rose, not moving.

'We can't stay here all night!'

Rose still did not budge.

'Oh, all *right!*' said Indigo in exasperation. 'I'll go and pinch it off the wall for you! Just this once! Never again!'

'No, never again,' agreed Rose, cheering up with amazing speed and following as he led the way back into school and along the empty corridors to the scene of the crime.

'This is only because it's your first day!' he told her. 'You needn't think I'm doing it every time they stick a picture of yours up on the wall . . .'

'I shan't do any more pictures,' said Rose, pushing open the door of the Class 1 classroom (luckily empty). 'I shan't do anything else, ever. Not at school.'

'That's what you think! Where's this picture then? Is that it?'

'Yes. Do you like it?'

'Mmmm,' said Indigo, levering out the drawing pins. 'Not bad. Bit like a banana. There you are. Roll it up! Oy! Wait for me!'

Rose did not wait, but sprinted out of school as fast as she could and was well on her way down the road home before Indigo caught up with her.

'What about in the morning?' he asked as they half jogged and half walked along together. 'What'll you tell them if they notice?'

'I could not go back in the morning,' said Rose hopefully, but Indigo squashed that idea at once. For a while he walked along frowning, with his hands in his pockets.

'I know,' he said suddenly, looking up. 'We'll make a copy! They can have that! Easy, especially if Saffron and Caddy help!'

'Saffron won't,' said Rose, and Saffron wouldn't.

'You'll never get away with it!' she said, after one look at the banana. 'No one could copy that! They'll see it's the wrong one straight away!'

' 'Course they won't,' said Caddy, now eighteen and at college, supposed to be passing a few exams. 'Give it here, Rose! I'll do it for you.'

Caddy's copy was perfect, down to four drawing pin holes in the corners.

'Just in case anyone catches you with it before you get it up on the classroom wall,' she explained. 'If I didn't put them in it would be obvious at once that you were planting a fake. Mind you use the same holes when you pin it up!'

Indigo and Rose looked at her with respect. Caddy could be surprisingly intelligent, considering how many exams she had failed.

Everything went exactly to plan. Indigo and Rose left for school extra early the next morning and pinned the copy of the Banana House in place, and nobody ever spotted the difference.

'You think you are all so clever,' said Saffron.

'You could have helped,' Rose pointed out. 'You didn't want to help.'

'No, I didn't,' snapped Saffron, crossly.

'It doesn't matter anyway,' said Rose tranquilly, admiring her picture for the hundreth time through half-closed eyes. 'Because I've got it safe now. It just needs framing . . . a big gold frame . . .'

'What needs a big gold frame?' asked Eve, coming through the door in time to catch Rose's last words. 'Your picture, Rose? Why don't you ask Daddy when he comes home next. He's good at frames. Saffy darling, I came in to ask you to hurry back from school tomorrow. Grandad's coming for the evening.'

'Grandad doesn't *only* like Saffron!' said Rose.

'Of course he doesn't,' said Eve.

'I need a big gold frame *now*, not when Daddy comes home!'

'I might have one in the shed you could use.'

'Grandad likes all of us, just the same.'

'Of course he does,' agreed Eve, soothingly, and she smiled at Saffron over Rose's head.

Saffron's black mood slipped away and she found herself smiling back, and she said to Rose,

'Of course he likes us all just the same.'

Their grandfather was in the kitchen when the children arrived home the next day. This pleased everyone. They all of them loved him, lately with a sort of fierce defiance, very like the way they had loved Rose years earlier, when she had been so frighteningly impermanent. They hurried to include him in their lives. Rose brought him the Banana House picture to look at, and he sat holding it in his thin hands for a long time before laying it on the table. Caddy told him about her driving lessons. Her father had arrived from London, inspected her exam results (appalling) and announced that it was about time Caddy learned to work. He had enrolled her at college to resit everything she had failed, and booked her a course of driving lessons.

Caddy told her grandfather how good she was at emergency stops and how bad she was at everything else, especially reversing, which she called going backwards.

Her grandfather looked as if he was listening.

'Feel that!' said Indigo, pulling up his sweatshirt sleeve and putting his grandfather's hand on his almost visible biceps, and his grandfather appeared to feel it. Indigo was very pleased and went to find the picture of the ice axe he was saving up to buy.

'I want one too,' said Rose.

'When you are older,' said Indigo kindly.

Saffron did not bring anything to show her grandfather, or talk to him, or explain pictures of ice axes in catalogues. She just sat beside him. Saffron, who had grown up to be so fierce and alone, was always gentle with her grandfather.

Eventually Caddy kissed him goodbye and left for her driving lesson, with a hamster in her pocket for comfort. Eve came in from her shed at the bottom of the garden and tried to send Rose to bed.

'Without any supper?' asked Rose, and Eve said, 'Food, food, I forgot about food!'

Indigo (who by necessity was growing into a very brave cook) said, 'I am making fried corned beef sandwiches for everyone,' and then the evening became very noisy and smoky. Indigo cut his finger on the corned beef tin, and Rose had to bandage it because Caddy was out and Saffron wouldn't and Eve could not bear the sight of blood. After that there was a quarrel about who would eat bled-on sandwiches (Rose and Indigo) and who would rather starve (Saffron).

During the quarrel Eve suddenly said, 'Grandad's tired!'

Saffron looked at him then and saw how terribly faded he had become. He looked narrow and lost. All at once she began to cry. She put her arms round her grandfather and cried and cried and Eve said, 'Come on, Saffy. Let's take him home.'

Caddy's driving instructor was called Michael. He had been a wonderful surprise to Caddy the first time she met him. She had been expecting someone grey-haired and short-tempered and not at all nice. All her friends' driving instructors were like that.

Michael said to Caddy, 'Now Cadmium, we are coming up to a crossroads. I should like you to take the turn on the right.'

'Right,' said Caddy, happily, very pleased to be out with Michael again. 'I'll remember!'

'You should be slowing down. Look in your mirror.'

Caddy looked and said, 'I don't like this lipstick.'

'You don't need lipstick,' said Michael, who always found it very difficult to keep up a professional detachment where Caddy was concerned. 'You . . . Indicate! Indicate!'

'Too pink,' said Caddy.

'TURN *RIGHT*, CADMIUM PLEASE!'

'But it was free. It came through the door. A little tiny one. So I thought I'd try it . . .'

'I said RIGHT! Crikey! Pull up and park immediately, please Caddy. *Please* Caddy!'

'. . . on you,' said Caddy, parking very neatly in an entrance marked KEEP CLEAR AT ALL TIMES. 'What's the matter? Are you all right?'

Caddy had driving lessons twice a week. She had had dozens. After every lesson Michael had to drive off and find somewhere quiet where he could rest his head on the steering wheel and try to relax. He didn't know why he put up with it, and yet every week he found himself coming back for more.

'*Are* you all right?' asked Caddy. 'No, you're not! You're cross! Again!'

'I'm not,' said Michael. 'Please change places, Cadmium dear.'

Caddy jumped out of her seat with relief, and back in at the passenger door. Michael turned the car very quickly and headed back the way they had come.

'What do you notice about this street?' he asked conversationally.

'Lovely gardens,' said Caddy, getting out her hamster.

'It's one way! Turn right, I said and instead you turned left up a one way street! Then you parked in the fire station exit. And that mirror is for looking *behind you*, not admiring your lipstick in!'

'I wasn't! I said it was too pink!'

'And I told you not to bring that hamster again!'

'Why are you stopping?'

'So you can drive. Your dad pays me to teach you to drive.'

'That reminds me,' said Caddy. 'Don't laugh. I promised him I'd ask you, but don't laugh. My driving test. He said to ask you when. That's all. You're laughing. I knew you would.'

'You could learn if you tried,' said Michael, when Caddy was back in the driving seat and he, much against his better judgment, was holding the hamster. 'You just need to stop mucking about and concentrate a bit.'

'That's what they used to tell me at school,' said Caddy. 'I remember them saying it before my GCSEs. And it wasn't true. It didn't work. I got awful grades in nearly everything. Biology, Chemistry, Physics, Maths, English Lang., English Lit., French and Business Studies. Awful. And last summer I failed all three 'A' levels. All three. I'm just no good at exams. Is it time to go home?'

'No. Twenty minutes. We'll do some reversing.'

'Oh, Michael *darling*!'

'Don't call me darling, I'm a driving instructor!'

'Sorry. It was because I hate going backwards.'

'My girlfriend,' said Michael suddenly, as Caddy reversed up a kerb, 'passed her test when she was seventeen!'

'Your girlfriend?'

'Yep.'

'I didn't know you had a girlfriend.'

'Yep. Very bright. Passed all her exams too. Top grades.'

'What's she called?'

'What?'

'What's she called?'

'Oh, right. Er . . . Diane. Diane.'

'I'll try the corner again,' said Caddy, gritting her teeth.

'She leaves her hamsters at home too,' said Michael.

The first thing Caddy and Michael saw when they arrived back from the driving lesson was Indigo.

'Just look at that stupid kid!' exclaimed Michael, absolutely horrified. 'No, don't jump out, Caddy! Don't startle him!'

Indigo was sitting on his bedroom windowsill. On the outside of his bedroom windowsill, the open window behind him, his legs dangling into space and his eyes looking like two black holes in his white face.

'I'm calling the fire brigade,' muttered Michael to Caddy, searching feverishly through his pockets. 'Where's my mobile? Are you sitting on it?'

'No, and calm down! Michael darling,' said Caddy, soothingly. 'You don't need to call anyone! Indigo often sits up there. He is curing himself of vertigo for when he becomes a polar explorer. It's a big wide windowsill and he has the curtains to hold on to. They're very strong. I tested them. He's waiting for me to talk him back. He freezes.'

'Freezes?'

'With fear. So I'd better go. Thank you for the lovely lesson. Bye bye, Michael.'

'Bye, Caddy.'

Michael waited as she disappeared into the house and reappeared at Indigo's window. He watched Indigo slowly defrost and begin to move. One leg swung back inside. Caddy's voice came floating down.

'Now the other leg. You're perfectly safe. Don't look down. Look at me!'

A moment later, and Indigo was back inside and was waving cheerfully from the window with Caddy and Rose, who had also appeared. Michael suddenly felt very left out, and drove quickly away.

Chapter Three

For nearly ten years the Casson children's grandfather had lived in his nursing home. When he first moved in there had not been space in his little room for all his belongings, and a lot of them had been stored in the Banana House.

One of these was a small box of books, about half a dozen. They were pushed under Indigo's bed (with a lot of other stuff) and they stayed there untouched for several years.

They were all books on the same subject and the subject was polar exploration. They were old, old books, with black and white photographs as illustrations. The photographs were of ice and cliffs, penguins and huskies, churning seas, deep snow, and wide horizons. There were also pictures of explorers, strong as steel and brave as tigers. When Indigo was little he used to drag the box out from under his bed and look at the photographs. He used to look at the polar explorers and think about his father.

None of the polar explorers were anything like his father.

Later Indigo learned to read. He managed this

much faster than Saffy because he had a reason for wanting to learn. Soon he could read the titles under the pictures. Then the chapter headings. Then all the short paragraphs in the pages opposite the pictures. By the time Saffron was reading the paint chart, Indigo (two years younger) was reading the books.

At first he read them very slowly, skipping huge chunks of text and all the footnotes, backtracking, misunderstanding, taking hours sometimes to sort through a couple of pages. It took him nearly two years to read the whole box.

The second time through was much faster. The third time was no struggle at all. The fourth and fifth and sixth times were as easy as breathing. He cross-referenced and checked maps and not a footnote escaped him. The polar world became as familiar as the Banana House.

Right from the beginning Indigo was fascinated by the lives of the polar explorers. Their cold, limitless world was the exact opposite of his own muddled home. Nobody Indigo knew had such adventures. He used to go through all the people he could think of, and picture them out on the ice, and reluctantly conclude that not one of them could stick it. They were none of them as strong as steel and as brave as tigers, and the least strong and brave of all of them (as Indigo knew only too well) was Indigo himself.

Indigo thought about it, and it seemed to him that he had been born afraid of almost everything.

He made a list. He wrote down on a piece of paper

all the things that frightened him most, and he set about to cure himself.

That was why he sat on his bedroom windowsill, frightening Michael and worrying Caddy, who only partly understood.

'I have to stop being afraid of heights,' said Indigo, trying to explain to her when Michael had been waved out of sight, and Rose had disappeared to visit Eve in her shed. 'In one of my books it says you should always do the things that frighten you most, and if you do them enough, they stop being scary. And I think it's true. So that's what I do. Listen! There's the telephone!'

'Perhaps it's Michael,' said Caddy hopefully, starting down the stairs to answer it. 'Perhaps he's found his mobile and suddenly remembered he forgot to ask me out! He's got our number . . . I keep giving it to him . . . Hello! Hello! . . . Oh!'

'Is it Michael?' asked Indigo, who had followed her down.

'No. It's Grandad's nursing home. Oh Indigo. Run out to the shed quickly and fetch Mum.'

Once again the children's father was forced to rush home from London midweek. This time (and it could not have been more inconvenient) it was because the children's grandfather, Eve's father, had died. Bill was not pleased to be summoned home, and although he would never have been tactless enough to say so outright, he could not see the urgency at all.

'He's dead! He's dead!' moaned Eve down the phone.

'Well, exactly,' said her husband. 'If you had let me know sooner . . . although even then I don't know what I could have done . . . but I really *can't* see, Eve darling, how me rushing away can be of any help . . . Are you listening?'

'Yes,' sobbed Eve.

'Good,' said her husband, and went on to explain (very patiently and kindly) how difficult it was for a real artist to prepare for an exhibition of their work, if they were constantly dragged away to deal with every minor crisis.

Eve could not seem to understand. She wailed down the phone, and Caddy wailed too, and so did Rose. Indigo would only say, 'When are you coming? When are you coming?' and Saffron refused to speak at all.

'Darling Eve,' said Bill patiently, 'it's not as if there was any great hurry any more!'

Of course, after that unfeeling remark he had to come home. The studio was shut up, the answer phone switched on, the milk and cream out of the fridge poured away, and all upright wine bottles were laid down on their sides (so that their corks did not dry out). Then e-mails needed to be dispatched to friends and fellow artists explaining that Bill Casson was out of town midweek, and a note written to the cleaning lady (who did not have e-mail) to remind her to water the plants. After that there was the two-hour train

31

journey home. Bill Casson grimly got out his lap-top and did his accounts and they made him even more depressed than ever. He decided Eve would have to pull herself together and economise.

There was no one to meet him at the station.

'Naturally I am sorry!' he said, when he arrived home to no supper, no hot water and his last week's laundry still untouched. '*Naturally* I am sorry the poor old boy has gone. At last. But some people might see it as all for the best. I think we should all try get this in perspective. And be sensible.'

Unfortunately his family had never been sensible. Far from it. They took no notice of his advice at all, and made no effort to get anything in perspective. Their grandfather was dead, and they had loved him. They felt as if they had lost a battle they might have won if only they had tried a bit harder. Not one of them would listen to reason, not even Indigo. Indigo's father thought that Indigo really might have had more sense, being a boy.

Indigo said, 'He wasn't even ill! There was nothing wrong with him!'

'Good grief, Indigo!' said his father in astonishment. 'He'd had two huge heart attacks! He hadn't *spoken* for nearly ten years . . .'

'He had!' interrupted Saffron, angrily. 'He said, "Saffron". Everyone heard!'

'It was amazing he carried on as long as he did,' continued Bill, tolerantly ignoring Saffron's rudeness. 'Anyway, he would not want you to be sad . . .'

Caddy, Saffron, Indigo and Rose stared at him as if he was mad.

'. . . and *I* am here now. You have *me*. I understand completely how you are feeling. I have closed up the studio and will stay until after the funeral . . .'

Eve put her hands over her ears, and Caddy said dolefully, 'I hate the thought of Grandad's funeral. I wish we could just bury him in the garden like the darling guinea pigs.'

Her father said not to be ridiculous, and anyway, she did not have to think of the funeral, no one expected her to go . . .

Saffron looked relieved and Caddy began to argue, and Eve wept, 'Whatever will we do without him?'

'Oh really, Eve!' snapped Bill, cross at last. 'You never did anything *with* him! You know as well as I do that the poor old chap had totally lost his marb . . .'

He was stopped by Saffron, who launched herself upon him, beating his chest with her bony fists while tears streamed down her cheeks.

'Sorry! Sorry! Sorry!' he exclaimed, detaching her before she could do any damage to his jacket (pale grey suede and very easily marked). 'Just a slip! I shouldn't have said that! Now, I think you people would all feel better for a good night's sleep! Why don't you take them up, Eve darling, while I find myself some supper. Where's that big apron I got you for Christmas?'

That was a good question to ask. It brought Eve to her senses. She jumped guiltily and pulled herself together enough to tell a small white lie for the sake of peace and quiet.

'Bedside table,' she said, even managing a sodden but definite smile. 'In my special drawer. Too pretty to mess up.'

'Silly Eve,' said her husband indulgently and Eve sighed with relief. She had given her Christmas apron (Monet's *Lily Pond* and waterproof) to Caddy, who had used it to control the seepage from her largest guinea pig hutch.

Upstairs Caddy said with great determination, 'I shall go to the funeral. I don't care what anyone else expects. *I* expect me to go.'

'Oh Caddy,' said Saffron miserably.

'I know. It's awful. But I'm going. We all should.'

'It will be so sad.'

'You have to be sad sometimes,' said Caddy. 'Whatever Dad says. He may be right. Grandad probably *had* totally lost his marbles, but I am still sad and I'm going to the funeral. I shall be as unhappy as I like and I shall wear black.'

All at once Saffron realised that Caddy was right. They should go, all of them. She said, 'I've got a black skirt. The one with the bead fringe that I got sent home from school in. And Indigo's got a black tee shirt, and his old black jeans. What about Rose?'

Rose, who had been pretending to be asleep, bobbed up and said, 'I shall wear my party dress.'

Caddy and Saffron nodded. They approved of

Rose's party dress. They had chosen it themselves and bought it out of the housekeeping money, which in the Banana House was kept handily in a jam jar on the kitchen mantelpiece.

Caddy had said, 'Rose ought to have a proper dress.'

They had chosen sequinned black velvet and silver taffeta. It cost one hundred and ten pounds.

Bill Casson, who had gone ahead to the church to make sure that everything was arranged to be as efficient and unexciting as possible, nearly passed out as his family filed in for their grandfather's funeral.

Rose in her silver skirts led the way, followed by Indigo in faded jeans, and Saffron, tinkling with beads. Saffron's bright gold hair streamed down her back like a tangled fleece, but Caddy's was piled high and bravely on the top of her head, and her dress (bought after all for driving lessons, not funerals) was very tight and very, very short. Eve staggered after them, clutching a box of mansize tissues, a hip flask of cough medicine, and a large bunch of daffodils which she intended to scatter in the grave.

'Eve *darling!*' hissed her husband furiously.

'Don't they look beautiful?' said Eve, taking a swig of cough medicine and then dragging a mansize tissue out of the box and wiping her eyes. 'Rose says we must all sing very loudly so that Grandad can hear us in heaven.'

They did sing very loudly, dark Casson eyes glued to the coffin, clear, unmusical Casson voices defiantly quenching the mumble of the rest of the congregation and the drone of the traffic outside. Saffron found herself unexpectedly happy. For a little while, a few minutes, she felt part of the family. Not an outsider. It didn't last long.

Their grandfather's will had been sent to the house, but no one except the children's parents had seen it.

'No reason why they should,' said their father briskly.

'It's a nice will,' said Eve.

'It's a very nice will,' agreed Bill kindly. 'Put it somewhere out of sight.'

Eve stuffed it behind the clock, which was only a small one and already expected to conceal an unreasonable number of brown envelopes. The will bulged out on either side, far from out of sight. On the Sunday after the funeral, in the empty spell between Sunday lunch and the arrival of the taxi that would take Bill back to the station (never Eve's most sensible time) she made the huge mistake of fishing it out.

'I suppose the children might as well hear what he wrote,' said their father. 'Even though it means nothing. It's out of date. He hadn't a bean by the time he died. Went through the lot. Poor old boy.'

Saffron stared at the will with a strange sort of beating in her heart. She had not thought of such a thing existing. Of all of them, she had felt their grandfather's death the most. He had been especially hers. He was the one who had brought her from

Siena. Hers was the name he had remembered, when everyone else's had been forgotten.

Perhaps it held a message from him. Saying not just 'Saffron', this time, but, 'Saffron. I loved you best. Here is the proof.'

That was what she longed for. Proof.

The will was ten years old. Caddy had been eight when it was written and Indigo a baby, just able to stand and wave out of the window at his grandfather's car. Rose would not arrive for another five years.

It was a will for the grandchildren.

To Cadmium Gold, my eldest grandchild, my property in Wales.

'That was the house on the cliff,' said Eve. 'We used to go there for summer holidays. You loved it Caddy. Your grandfather promised it to you even then . . .'

'He was joking, Eve,' said her husband patiently.

'Anyway, it went a long time ago,' said Eve sighing. 'We had to sell it after he got ill . . .'

'It was crumbling away,' said Bill. 'And so was the cliff it was standing on. Nobody has ever really lived there. It was worth next to nothing. I told him so when he bought it but he took absolutely no notice of me . . . Never did.'

To Indigo Charles, my car.

'His Bentley,' remembered Eve. 'Indigo could pick that car out from any other car in the road when he was only ten months old!'

'What happened to it?' asked Indigo.

'Wrote it off when he had that first heart attack,' said his father. 'I saw it myself afterwards. They took it back to his house. Absolute wreck. We couldn't claim a penny. It wasn't insured as it should have been. I did warn him, several times. History now.'

> *To any further grandchildren, born to Eve and Bill Casson after the date of this will, my remaining capital to be divided evenly between them.*

'That's Rose, you see,' explained Bill, 'because it says "*After*". Grandchildren born after the date of the will. If there was any remaining capital it would go to Rose. But unfortunately . . .'

'Capital,' remarked Rose from under the table where she often took refuge in times of crisis. 'What's capital?'

'Money,' said Indigo. 'You'd get money.'

'Money!' repeated Rose in disgust. 'I've got money! I've got that money Dad gave me when he came back from America. It's no use at all!'

'I *explained* to you, Rose, that it was American money,' said her father patiently. '*And* I brought you back that lovely rabbit. Anyway . . .'

'That rabbit had pants made out of a flag,' said Rose scornfully.

'The *American* flag,' said her father. 'That was why.

I've explained before, Rose! I don't know how many times! Anyway . . .'

'Flags are flags and pants are pants,' said Rose.

'*Anyway . . .*'

'Flag pants!'

'*ANYWAY . . .*' Bill said very loudly, 'that's the end of your grandfather's will. Such as it was. Except for some odds and ends . . .'

'But what about Saffron?' demanded Caddy.

'There's a note about Saffron. I was coming to that next.'

Saffron's note was not part of the will at all. It was a sheet of notepaper, pinned to the back with a rusty pin. Bill unpinned it and handed it to her.

It was not typed, but written in black ink, in handwriting that Saffy did not recognise but guessed must be her grandfather's. It was very shaky.

For Saffron. Her angel in the garden.

Then there were three more words, not very clear.

'For Saffron,' read Saffron. 'Her angel in the garden. The stone angel.'

'Well,' said Bill, getting up very briskly. 'There we are. Very kind. He thought of you all. But there's nothing. House went years ago. He finished off the car himself. Absolutely no capital. Poor old boy. Still . . .'

'But what about my angel?' demanded Saffron, clutching her note, the words bursting from her. 'My angel. The angel in the garden. The stone angel. Where's my angel?'

'Saffy, Saffy, Saffy,' said Bill, laughing. 'That was just a note. Wandering. Not even witnessed. Wouldn't be legal whatever it was . . .'

Eve did not laugh. She put an arm round Saffy and said, 'I suppose he was thinking of a sort of guardian angel, Saffy darling. Because I think he must have written that note just after your mother had died. Don't you think so? Something like that . . . Not a real angel. Well, yes, a real angel . . . But not a thing. That's what I mean. Not a thing. A thought.'

'A *stone* angel, it says,' said Saffron. 'Anyway, Caddy had the house. That was real.'

'Yes, but it's gone now,' said Eve.

'But he thought it was real,' persisted Saffron. 'He meant it to be real. And Indigo had his car, and that was real as well. And I suppose he thought there would be some money, even if there wasn't, so Rose's bit is real too. So there must be an angel! He was my grandfather too! He wouldn't leave me out!'

'He didn't know you as well as he knew Caddy and Indigo,' said Eve, choosing her words very carefully. 'Not at first. Not when he wrote that will. You were in Italy, you see, and they were in England. That visit he made to Siena when your mother died was the first time he'd seen you . . . don't cry Saffy . . .'

'It's always different for me!' sobbed Saffy. 'It's not fair! He was my grandfather just as much as theirs!'

'Saffron, it's just the same for all of you,' said Bill as patiently as he could manage. 'Look at Caddy and Indigo and Rose! They're not getting upset like this. Nor your mother . . .'

'She's not my . . .' began Saffy stormily, and then swallowed the words. After all, it wasn't Eve's fault.

Bill was looking at his watch, the way he did on Sundays. He had a special manner of doing it, sweeping his arm in a circle, shooting up his shirt sleeve, raising his eyebrows, and sighing. It was the signal for the official end of Sunday afternoon. Normal life was about to resume.

'Saffy darling, Daddy's got to go very soon,' said Eve. 'For his train. Poor Bill! So why don't we all . . .'

Saffron sniffed and pulled away . . .

'. . . wave?' said Eve, hopefully.

Rose, (Permanent Rose, heiress) came out from underneath the kitchen table and said very cheerfully, 'I *love* waving bye bye to Dad!'

'Rose!' said Eve reproachfully, and tried to push back her happiness at the thought that she would soon be in her lovely shed.

'I'll get his bag!' said Indigo, as relieved as everyone else that the tension seemed to be over. 'Caddy can look out the front for the taxi. Go and look for the taxi, Cad!'

'Come on, Saffron!' said Caddy, jumping up. 'When he's gone we can be properly miserable again. If we want to . . .'

Saffron looked around, and it seemed to her that the

Cassons were shaking off sadness like a dog shakes off water. Bill was saying,

'Well, well, back to the hard life! Give me a kiss, Rose! Jacket . . . wallet . . . mobile . . . lap–top . . . bag (thank you, Indigo)! Sandwiches, Eve darling? How sweet . . .'

'Taxi's here!' shouted Caddy from the front room window.

'Waving! Waving!' exclaimed Rose, and sped upstairs with Indigo after her.

'Saffy, be a good girl for your mother and give your old dad a kiss!'

'She's not my mother!' hissed Saffy, wriggling in his arms and furious with him because he was so cheerfully escaping them all. 'And you are not my dad and I hate you and I hope you never come . . .'

It was no good. Bill was not going to be provoked at his moment of release.

'You are our darling girl and we love you!' he said, laughing and picking up Saffy to swoop her down the front steps, just as he used to do when she was little and cried because he was leaving. 'And I know you don't hate me . . .' (He gave her two huge kisses, one on each cheek.)

'. . . and I will *always* come back!'

He had a charm about him sometimes, a warmth that was irresistible, like sunshine. He planted Saffy triumphantly on the pavement, opened the taxi door, slung in his bag, gave a huge film star wave, called, 'All right, Peter? Good weekend?' to the taxi driver who knew him well and considered him a lovely man, and was free.

'Back to the hard life,' he said to Peter, and stretched out his legs.

Back to the real life, he meant. The real world where there were no children lurking under the tables, no wives wiping their noses on the ironing, no guinea pigs on the lawn nor hamsters in the bedrooms, none but the most respectable of funerals, and no paper bags of leaking tomato sandwiches.

Saffron had the sandwiches. She stood in the street, lost between laughter and tears and found that at the last moment, after the darling girl, and the swoop down the steps and the hug and the film star wave, he had planted his sandwiches on her. He hated sandwiches. He always managed to leave them, and he always made it look like an accident.

Far down the road she could see the taxi, crawling along behind a milk float. There was still time to catch him.

Saffron began a sandwich chase. She began running after the taxi, tearing madly along the pavement, scattering sandwiches. This time, she thought, he would not escape.

He was still waving. He must have seen her. There was his head, leaning across to Peter, saying something.

The taxi went faster. It overtook the milk float and whizzed through the orange-turning-to-red traffic lights at the end of the road.

'I hate you! I hate you!' wailed Saffron, and flung the last of the sandwiches at the final glimpse of her father as he disappeared from view.

The milk float trundled past, rattling with empty bottles. It rattled over the tomato sandwiches so that they plastered themselves on to its wheels. Then the road was quiet again.

Saffron said aloud, 'I don't want to go home.'

As she spoke she became aware of a humming sound, getting louder. Next there was a flash of silver. Then something knocked into her, very hard, from behind.

'Where *is* everyone?' asked Caddy, when Rose came downstairs from waving.

'Mum, shed,' said Rose. 'I expect. Indigo, windowsill and you're not to go up to him yet, he said to tell you. He is dealing with extremes of fear.'

'What?'

'That's what he said,' said Rose, getting out mustard, tomato ketchup, curry powder and her paint book. ' "Tell Caddy I'm dealing with extremes of fear and not to come up till I shout." I'm painting an eatable picture. What can I use to make blue?'

'Blue Smarties,' suggested Caddy.

'Haven't got any.'

'You could mix blue paint into something. Like mayonnaise.'

'Blue paint's cheating.'

'Toothpaste,' said Caddy triumphantly. 'Blue gel

toothpaste. We've got some in the bathroom. And red wine makes a lovely purple. There's still a bit left in that bottle by the sink. You could use that.'

'Marmite for brown,' said Rose. 'Toothpaste and mustard for green.'

'Do you know where Saffy is, Rose?'

'Mmmm?'

'Saffy. Do you know where she is?'

Rose was already half lost in her painting, but she dragged herself far enough back again to answer Caddy.

'Run off,' she said, poking a large paint brush into the Marmite. 'After Dad. Chucking sandwiches. Screaming. Got squashed flat by that girl in the wheelchair.'

'Is she hurt? Is she OK?'

'*I* don't know,' said Rose. 'Anyway, you can't go out, Indigo might fall out of the window. She looked all right to me.'

Chapter Four

Saffron sat up on the pavement and rubbed her knees. Then she pushed up her sleeve and twisted her right arm round to inspect her elbow. It was bleeding a little. She felt very tired. As if she had been running and shouting and crying for a long time.

The girl in the wheelchair who had knocked her over was watching intently.

'Speak!' she ordered at last, when it seemed that Saffron intended to sit there for ever.

Saffron folded her arms across her hunched up knees and rested her head on them.

'I know you,' said the girl, spinning backwards on one wheel like a gyroscope. 'You come from that house where they're always waving. Did I hurt you?'

'No.'

'Aren't you going to get up?'

'Soon I will.'

'Why are they always waving from your house?'

'I don't know.'

'Why were you shouting at your father like that? Do you really hate him?'

'No,' said Saffron, and then added, 'he's not my father. I'm adopted.'

'Are you all adopted?' asked the girl, still revolving, but more slowly now. 'The others, too? The grown-up girl who looks like you, and the little one and the boy?'

'No,' said Saffron. 'Only me.'

The girl in the wheelchair took a long look at Saffron. It was a very careful look. Her eyes, silvery green like light on deep water, were wide and intense.

'I know your name,' she announced. 'You're Saffron Casson. Saffron. And you've a sister called Caddy . . .'

'Cadmium. She's my cousin really.'

'. . . and another called Rose. The little one. And the dark-haired boy is called Indigo . . .'

'How do you know our names?'

'. . . and you've all been walking past me for years and years and years . . .'

'Is that why you bashed me over?'

'. . . without saying a word . . .'

'*Is* that why?'

'. . . without even looking at me . . .'

'I didn't think it was an accident!'

'. . . just as if I wasn't there!'

Saffron thought about that and then said, 'Sorry,' which was not a word she used very much. 'What are we going to do now?' she asked, and inside she wondered, Friends or Enemies? Obviously it would have to be one or the other. She was quite sure this girl who had knocked her over would never settle for anything in between.

The girl suddenly smiled and her face became lit and sparkling. Saffron felt her friendliness like the warmth of a fire.

'You could just keep on walking past, not looking at me.'

'No,' said Saffron at once. 'I've done that. Something else.'

'You could chuck sandwiches at me and I could bash you over.'

'Yes, all right,' said Saffron, and she felt happier than she had for ages.

She had never had a proper friend. There had been girls she got on with at school but outside school they had never bothered about her much. Saffron had managed without being too lonely because at home she always had Caddy, who was friends with all the world, and Indigo, who cared for no one but his pack. Those two, with Eve and Rose and her grandfather and Bill (now and then) had been all the people with a place in her life.

'I don't know your name,' she said, as they went along the road together.

'Sarah,' said the girl, and Saffy said, 'Oh yes,' as if it was a name that she had known all along, but forgotten for a moment.

Now that they were friends she could look at Sarah's wheelchair properly for the first time, and she realised that it was not the one she had carefully avoided seeing for so many years.

'You've got a new one,' she said, surprised. 'A new wheelchair. Haven't you?'

Sarah looked pleased.

'It's a sports one,' she told Saffron, and rushed off ahead for a minute in a series of swerving swoops.

'I can do skids,' she said, swooping back again, but not knocking Saffron over this time. 'And handbrake turns. Nearly. And I can go fast . . . have you got a bike?'

'No,' said Saffron.

'Wouldn't you like one?'

'Yes. So would Indigo.'

'Have you got roller blades?'

'No.'

'A skateboard?'

'No,' said Saffron regretfully.

'I would like all those things,' said Sarah. 'Fast things. You wait till I learn to drive! I'm going to have a bright red open-top two-seater sports car.'

Saffron opened her mouth to point out the probable impossibility of this and then shut it again.

'There's no reason why I shouldn't,' said Sarah crossly, guessing Saffron's thoughts, and then went very fast for a bit so that Saffy had to run to catch up.

'I didn't say anything!'

'You were going to, though!' said Sarah. 'Tell me why you chucked sandwiches at your dad.'

'What, right from the beginning?'

Sarah nodded.

Saffy began with the most important thing, the stone angel, the angel in the garden. Sarah, recognising its importance, listened without interrupting, taking it all in.

Encouraged by her attention, Saffron went back a bit to describe her grandfather. Then forwards to the funeral. Then back again to Rose's party dress. Then on to Caddy and the exams she had failed and her guinea pigs and hamsters and the way she had copied the picture of Rose's Banana House, stolen by Indigo on Rose's first day of school.

'Indigo's a funny name,' said Sarah.

'Paint,' said Saffron, and then went far, far back, to the day she had finally learned to read and discovered her name was not on the colour chart on the kitchen wall.

'But are they all called after paint?' demanded Sarah. 'Caddy and Rose? Are they paint names too?'

'Oh yes,' said Saffron, 'Caddy is Cadmium Gold. That's a real colour. And Rose is a proper colour too. Permanent Rose and Rose Madder. They're both on the paint chart.'

'Permanent Rose!' said Sarah, beginning to laugh.

Saffron explained how impermanent Rose had seemed when she was born, and how she had eaten the paint (Yellow Ochre. Non-poisonous, now a family legend) when she was ten months old, and how they all thought it must have done her good because from that day onwards she had grown stronger and stronger.

'And more and more permanent!' said Saffron.

'Could it really have made her so much better?' asked Sarah in such an intensely interested voice that Saffron said hastily, 'No, no, no!' and hurried on to describe Eve's shed, but not Bill's studio, because she had never been there. However, she did mention his pale grey suede jacket and that brought her very quickly back to the sandwiches.

'I know about them,' said Sarah impatiently. 'Tell me about the angel again. The angel in the garden. The stone angel.'

'I don't know any more about it, except what I've already told you.'

'Well, tell me about the garden. No, not the guinea pig garden! The angel garden!'

'There isn't an angel garden,' began Saffron, 'there's only the guinea pig garden . . .'

Suddenly Saffron stood still in astonishment. All at once she understood. Of course there was an angel garden. She had known it for years. It was the one she remembered in her dreams.

She began to tell Sarah about the white stone garden with the little pointed trees in Siena, a long time ago.

Bill Casson left the train at King's Cross station and stepped into his London life as easily and contentedly as he would have stepped into a pair of old shoes (if he had had a pair of old shoes). Without knowing he was doing it he began to hum a song that he never hummed at home.

At the bottom of the Banana House garden, in her lovely shed, Eve was stretched out on her shabby pink sofa gazing at her latest painting (*Post Office on a Sunny Morning*). She was thinking of nothing. She was falling asleep.

In the kitchen of the Banana House Rose was totally absorbed in edible art. When Rose was engrossed in a picture the world could tumble to pieces around her head and she would not notice. Caddy was doing her college homework, sharing the kitchen table with Rose, and the entire contents of the fridge.

Indigo sat on his windowsill not coping with the extremes of fear very well at all. It was getting dark and his feet had gone to sleep from dangling too long. He knew by now that he had been forgotten. He was Indigo in the indigo dusk and he felt lost.

He thought, I should shout.

A proper shout meant taking a deep breath. He was much too frightened to do that. For a long time he had been so motionless it seemed to him the slightest change of position would throw him off balance. It occurred to him that he might have to stay there all night.

'Caddy!' he called, only it wasn't a call, it was just a small high sound like a bat might make.

'Caddy!' cried Indigo again.

No one could have heard it, and yet suddenly there

was the sound of footsteps on the stairs. Caddy grabbed him by the waist and pulled him inside so vigorously that they both went sprawling backwards on the threadbare carpet.

'Indigo, Indigo!' she wailed. 'I forgot you!'

'I thought you must have,' said Indigo, and he began to tremble.

'You're frozen! You must have been there hours.'

'Yes.'

'I was doing homework. That'll teach me! I am so, so, sorry!'

'It's not your fault.'

'I should have looked after you! I forgot! I don't know where Saffy is either! Do you?'

'No,' Indigo started to say, and then realised that he did know, and had known all the time that he had been sitting on the windowsill, unsuccessfully dealing with the extremes of fear. 'Yes I do! She's outside, with the wheelchair girl! She's been there for ages, going up and down. First to her house, then back to ours, then to hers again. They're talking and talking . . . Listen!'

Words were coming up through the open window. A clear voice saying:

'You ought to have it! You will have to find it! Think! Think where it could be!'

Caddy and Indigo looked at each other in astonishment.

'I wish I could remember better,' they heard Saffron reply. 'I wish I could remember more! Sometimes in

53

dreams I do, but I forget again. And nobody thinks there ever was an angel . . .'

'Everyone has something they have to do,' the clear voice interrupted firmly. 'And you have to find your angel. It's perfectly obvious. I will help you!'

'I'm going to fetch them in!' said Caddy. 'The wheelchair girl is absolutely right! If there really is an angel for Saffron somewhere, she ought to have it!'

Hurrying to the window she stuck her head out and called, 'Saffy! Saffy! Both of you! Come in!'

Saffy gave one startled look up at the house, seized Sarah's wheelchair and ran.

She knew quite well what would happen the moment she let Sarah meet her family. She would lose her. Sarah was just the sort of person that Caddy and Indigo and Rose would like. They would make friends immediately. Then Eve would come out of her shed and be sweet and useless and friendly, and she would like Sarah too. And sooner or later Bill would reappear from London and be efficient and handsome and make excellent jokes. Sarah would be swept away on a wave of Casson charm.

Saffron had lost her grandfather only the week before. She had lost her family twice, the first time in Italy, and the second time when she had discovered her name was not on the paint chart. She seemed to have been losing people all her life and she had no intention of losing the first proper friend she had ever made.

Back down the road to Sarah's home ran Saffron, and in at the drive of the house, without pausing once to look back.

'Stop!' roared Sarah, just in time.

Saffron stopped so hard at the front door that Sarah was nearly catapulted out. There was a doorbell and a knocker. Saffron attacked them both. When Sarah's mother arrived a moment later she thrust the wheelchair in past her legs, gasped, 'I'll call for you tomorrow!' and disappeared before either of them could say a word.

She was just in time. Running along the road towards her (as she had known they would be) were Caddy and Indigo and Rose, calling, 'Saffy! Saffy! Saffy!' like a flock of strange birds.

Saffron hurried back to the Banana House, answering questions as she ran.

'She had to go home. Her name's Sarah. She's got something wrong with her legs that she's had from a baby. She can walk. She says a wheelchair's faster. She goes to the private school where they have that blue and gold uniform. She's thirteen.'

'She could have come to supper,' said Caddy, as they arrived back in the jumbled kitchen. 'You should have asked her, Saffy!'

'No I shouldn't,' said Saffron. 'Anyway, what supper? Do you mean that stuff all over the table? Who'd want to eat that?'

Caddy explained that the stuff all over the kitchen table was Rose's Art, not supper, and that Indigo had said he would make toasted curry sandwiches, which were a speciality of his.

'I'm putting banana in them tonight,' said Indigo. 'Banana, raisins, curry and chicken. Clear the table, Rose!'

Rose ignored him and hung critically over her picture.

'It's the sort of thing,' she said thoughtfully, 'that I give away. Do you think the wheelchair girl would like it?'

'Sarah!' said Saffron. 'Don't keep calling her the wheelchair girl! Of course she wouldn't like it! What could she do with it? You don't know what to do with it yourself!'

'You shouldn't have used jam,' said Indigo, coming over from his cooking to inspect it. 'Jam's too sticky. You'll have to chuck it. How shall I make the curry? Very hot or very, very hot?'

'Very, very hot,' said Caddy. 'Might as well. Perhaps you could take your picture to school, Rose. And give it to your teacher.'

'She'd stick it on the wall,' said Rose. 'Flies would come and I'd have to look at it.'

'I don't see why you can't just throw it away,' remarked Indigo.

Rose explained that she never threw her art away, any more than Indigo ever threw his cooking away.

'We have to eat it,' she said, 'whatever it tastes like. And someone has to have my art, whatever it looks like. Or else it's a waste.'

'Post it to Dad!' said Saffron, suddenly inspired.

Arguing about whether or not this was a kind thing to do took up the rest of the evening. By the end of it only Saffron remembered their grandfather's will, stuffed once again behind the kitchen clock. When she went up to bed she took it with her and read again the tattered note in her grandfather's handwriting.

For Saffron. Her angel in the garden. The stone angel.

Sarah had said that everyone had something they ought to do, and Saffy ought to find her angel.

That night in her dreams she was in the white stone garden again, with the little pointed trees and the sound of water. Once more she walked hand in hand with someone, but this time she knew it was her grandfather. When she looked up she could see his face. It was tired and sad.

Saffron could also see her angel. It stood on a small white pedestal. She had known it all her life. It was her angel in the garden, and she had called it that in her mind ever since she could remember, long before she learned to say the words out loud.

Saffron's three-year-old world had fallen to pieces. Her mother had vanished, and everything she thought of as home was packed into her grandfather's car. Everything, that was, except her angel.

The dream went on, far past the point where it usually stopped, replaying in Saffron's mind the events of ten years before.

Saffron clings to her angel and cries and cries and her grandfather does something strange. He takes out a blue pencil and he writes on the angel. On the base, low down, so that Saffron can see.

'Look,' he says, and points and reads out what he has written.

'For Saffron' on one side of the base, and 'Saffy's Angel' on the other.

Saffron magically stops crying.

Her grandfather sighs and puts the pencil away and hopes that she will forget.

Chapter Five

'Michael darling,' said Caddy, dumping a very large box (which squeaked) in the back of Michael's car, 'Do not say a word! Ignore it! How is Droopy Di?'

Michael said, 'Mirror, signal, check your blind spot, and don't call me darling, I'm a driving instructor. It's another ruddy hamster, isn't it?'

'Nope,' said Caddy, pulling away very neatly and not needing any of Michael's instructions. 'Guinea pig. Pregnant. Babies any minute. I feel I have to be there. Left or right at the end of the road?'

'Left,' said Michael. 'Then we can do an emergency stop and drop it in the river. Indicate!'

'I am indicating! Do you like my new top?'

Michael allowed himself to look at Caddy for the first time since she had climbed into the car. It was a moment that he always put off for as long as possible because his concentration was never quite the same afterwards. He could not think of anything sensible to say about her new top. He bit back the words, 'You'll freeze.'

'Where are we going today?' asked Caddy. 'What about the dual carriageway? We haven't been there since I hit that squirrel!'

Michael groaned.

'You'll have to face it sometime,' said Caddy bracingly. 'They take you there on the driving test. A friend told me. Girl friend! Don't look like that, Michael! You know quite well there is only you!'

'Keep checking your mirror!'

'Only you,' repeated Caddy, dreamily. 'I knew for certain after the dual carriageway day. When you absolutely promised me that squirrels went to heaven . . . Are you *sure* squirrels go to heaven? Were you telling the truth?'

'No,' said Michael cheerfully. 'I only said it to stop you crying . . . HOLD ON TO THE STEERING WHEEL . . . Yes, yes, of course it is true . . . obviously they go there! Where else? Change gear . . . that's my leg . . .'

'Sorry,' said Caddy, recovering herself.

'Concentrate!'

'Yes, Michael. How's the brainy girlfriend? You haven't said a word.'

'What?' asked Michael. 'Oh, her. Yes, fine, thank you. Great form. Turn right at the roundabout.'

'What does she look like?'

'Oh,' said Michael, a bit taken aback. 'Well, you know, blonde. Blonder than you. Tallish.'

'Taller than me?'

'Oh yes.'

'Fantastically beautiful?'

'Absolutely,' said Michael, getting into the swing of the conversation. 'And, you know, intelligent looking.

And (of course) rodent free. Otherwise quite like you. Follow the signs for the dual carriageway then, if you are totally bent on destruction.'

'Darling Michael.'

'Start to get some speed up now.'

'If one of the baby guinea pigs looks like you I'll give it to you for a present.'

'Look for a gap in the traffic. Well done!'

'You can give it to Diane if you like.'

'Who?'

'Beautiful Di. Tell me if you hear a squeak.'

'Overtake that van in front now, Cadmium.'

'No,' said Caddy firmly. 'I can't do it. I'm not the overtaking sort, and anyway I wanted to talk to you about my brother Indigo. He nearly fell out of the window yesterday. I forgot him. I was doing homework, and I forgot him. That was your fault too, showing off about your brainy girlfriend! So, did you sit on windowsills when you were eleven, and if so, how did you stop?'

'I never did it. Sorry.'

'Has Droopy Di got little brothers?'

'Yes, but they don't sit on windowsills!'

'How many has she got?'

'How many have you got?'

'One. And two sisters.'

'She's got two,' said Michael. 'And four sisters!'

'Gosh!' said Caddy. 'All right, I will overtake! There! Wasn't that brilliant? Is she the eldest?'

'It was very neat indeed,' said Michael kindly. 'Even

61

Droopy Di couldn't have done it better. Yes, she is the eldest. Takes care of them all. Mother's useless.'

'And she's passed all those exams?'

'Standing on her head,' said Michael smugly. 'She's at university now.'

'What doing?'

Michael glanced sideways at Caddy and made a guess.

'Zoology.'

Caddy did an emergency stop on the fast lane of the dual carriageway. The guinea pig box fell off the seat and there was a tremendous hooting from behind.

'WHAT THE . . . WHY THE . . . WHY ON *EARTH* DID YOU DO THAT?' demanded Michael, making humble praying gestures to the driver that had missed them (now leading a long train of overtakers, all expressing their feelings as they passed). 'Good grief, look at the traffic! Start the engine, Caddy! *Start* the engine! All right, stay there while I come round . . . Now slide over!'

Caddy slid over and sat very quietly while Michael drove them away. He did not say anything, and neither did she, until they were nearly home.

Then he said, 'That was so stupid!'

'I know. Sorry.'

'What was it then? Another squirrel?'

Caddy shook her head.

'What then?'

'Droopy Di,' said Caddy miserably.

'*Droopy Di?*'

'She is doing exactly what I wanted to do!' burst out Caddy. 'Before I failed all those exams! When I was still at school. When I was young . . .'

'How old are you now?'

'Eighteen. I was going to study zoology and then go to Africa and work in one of those national parks. People do. I thought I could.'

'Lions and things?'

'Wouldn't it be lovely?'

'You'd have good weather anyway.'

'Is that what Diane's going to do?'

'No,' said Michael firmly, deciding that Diane had had enough good fortune for one afternoon. 'She's never mentioned lions to me. Never.'

'She could do though, if she wanted.'

'So could you,' pointed out Michael. 'Do your exams, get yourself into university. What's to stop you?'

Caddy looked at him in astonishment.

'You want to get yourself thinking straight,' advised Michael, pulling up outside Caddy's house. 'Same goes for your brother! There's a climbing wall at the gym in town. Tell him he wants to go there and learn properly, instead of mucking about on windowsills!'

'Michael darling,' said Caddy. 'You are a great brain! I'm sorry I stopped on the dual carriageway like that. It was shock.'

'Shocked me too,' said Michael. 'If you do it again I will dump you. Somebody else will have to teach you. You'll need to be able to drive in Africa. Land Rovers, probably. Somebody wants you! See them waving?'

He watched as Caddy fished behind the seat for her box and climbed out of the car. Rose came running from the house to meet her, holding out a large wet picture that flapped.

'Lovely!' said Caddy, taking it carefully. 'It's me! Look, Michael!'

'Lovely,' agreed Michael, and drove away quite reluctantly thinking, lovely, lovely.

Sarah's mother opened the door to Saffron looking not at all pleased. She was tall and tidy and very, very efficient looking. She said, 'Saffron, isn't it?'

'Yes,' replied Saffron, suddenly nervous. 'I've come to call for Sarah. Is she in?'

'You kept her out far too late last night,' said Sarah's mother, not smiling. 'She gets tired.'

'I didn't know.'

'She's doing her homework at the moment. Have you finished yours?'

'Oh,' said Saffron. 'Homework. Well, no. I do it on the bus. Usually.'

Saffron could feel panic setting in. There was something Sarah had told her about her mother the night before that she could not remember. Something important, to do with school.

'*On the bus?*'

'I go to the comprehensive,' said Saffron meekly.

'Not the rich ki . . . not the other school. So homework doesn't matter. As much.'

'It's an excellent comprehensive,' said Sarah's mother. 'Homework always matters. We think.'

All at once Saffron remembered what it was about Sarah's mother. She was Mrs Warbeck. The headmistress of the private school. The rich kids' school. That was it. Saffron had known it was something terrible.

'Perhaps you would like to have supper with us?' Mrs Warbeck was asking Saffron now. 'After Sarah has finished her homework? You could telephone your mother from here if you like. Or pop back home. Would she mind?'

Saffron shook her head.

'We get our own supper,' she said. 'And anyway, it's no good telephoning. She'll be in the shed.'

'*In the shed?*'

The face of Sarah's mother said as plainly as if she had spoken that Eve should not be in the shed. She should be cooking. This was the hour of the day when respectable mothers cooked for their respectable families, while supervising homework.

Saffron, feeling hopelessly unrespectable, looked around for a way of escape. Astonishingly, she found one. It was on the wall. A picture by her mother. *Town Bridge on a Bright Evening*. She said, 'My mother painted that!'

'Did she?' asked Mrs Warbeck. 'Did she *really*? Why, of course! It's an Eve Casson! How silly of me not to realise!' and she looked at Saffron in quite a different, much more friendly, kind of way.

'She paints in the shed,' explained Saffron, and Sarah's mother said, 'Of course!' and smiled at Saffron, and asked if she was artistic too, and wasn't her father Bill Casson also an artist, and said how exciting it must be to be one of such a creative family. Before Saffron could decide whether to agree (Yes, very exciting!), or tell the truth (No, not at all, and they're not my parents, I'm adopted), Sarah herself appeared, coming down the stairs.

'My soufflé!' exclaimed Mrs Warbeck, and disappeared through a door.

'I heard her booming away,' said Sarah, grinning. 'I'd have come sooner if I'd known it was you!'

'Shall I help you?' asked Saffron shyly. Sarah on her legs, instead of in a wheelchair, looked terribly frail. She moved as if the world was in danger of slipping away beneath her feet.

'Help me what?' asked Sarah. 'Oh, walk! No thanks. You can help me with my homework if you like though! Are you any good at French?'

'No.'

'Science?'

'No.'

'Maths?'

'No.'

'Oh well,' said Sarah cheerfully. 'Never mind! Come back upstairs to my bedroom till it's suppertime.'

'But you've just come down!' protested Saffron.

'Don't fuss!' commanded Sarah. 'Mum fusses, Dad fusses. They fuss at school, they fuss at the hospital. Everyone I crash into with my wheelchair fusses. Don't you start! Have you found your angel yet?'

'No,' said Saffron, not fussing, as Sarah started on another flight of stairs, 'but I think I know where it is. Italy. Siena, where I was born. I had a dream and saw it there. Why is your bedroom right at the top of the house?'

'That's where I chose,' said Sarah.

'Do you always get your own way?'

'Nearly,' admitted Sarah. 'My mother is tough, but I am tougher and Dad isn't tough at all. So I win. You will have to get to Siena somehow then, if that's where your angel is. Mind the drum kit!'

'I'm trying to think of a way,' said Saffron, stepping round the drum kit. 'I've got a passport, that's a start. Why have you got all this stuff?'

'Everyone's got stuff,' said Sarah.

'Two computers!'

'I only use one of them.'

'Two guitars, *and* a keyboard!'

'Well, you can't play the drums all the time!'

'TV, music centre, what's that thing for?'

'Lighting system!'

'Why've you got kites hanging all over the ceiling?'

'I just have. I like them.'

'Ten thousand teddy bears!'

'I used to collect them!'

'Is that a fridge?'

'Only a little one!'

'Why do you need two beds?'

'I get bored easily.'

'*And* a hammock!'

'I just use that for shoving things in!'

'Have you read all those books? What do you look at with that telescope? I've never seen so many CDs!'

'OK! Shut up now, Saffron!'

'I've always wanted a chair like this! I love swivel chairs! Is that whole crate full of nail varnish? Nothing else but nail varnish!'

'All right,' said Sarah. 'I've got a lot of stuff. Don't look at it. It's only stuff. Everyone has it.'

'Not like this,' said Saffron. 'Where does it all come from?'

'Parents, grandparents,' said Sarah, a little impatiently. 'Come on Saffron! Don't pretend your family don't give you stuff!'

Saffron thought about what her family gave her. Food. Necessary clothes. Christmas dolls and teddies and books when she was little. The right sort of trainers for her last birthday, undoubtedly chosen by Caddy. Nothing at all like Sarah's collection.

'Your grandfather,' said Sarah, 'has given you an *angel*! An angel! Stop being sorry for yourself!'

Saffron said indignantly that she was not being sorry for herself, and added that she would never in a thousand years want stuff like Sarah's, and could not understand why anyone would. Then there was very nearly a quarrel and the words, Rich Kids' School,

Jealous, and Spoilt Only Child hung unspoken in the air between them.

'And,' said Saffron vehemently, as if they had all been said, 'it's nothing to do with you about my angel! I wish I'd never told you!'

'But you did,' said Sarah calmly. 'So too late! I'll help you find it, too. I said I would. I always do what I say I will.'

'You can mind your own business,' began Saffron hotly, and would have said more if just then Sarah's mother had not called that supper was ready.

'Pot luck,' she said, mystifying Saffron, who had never heard these modest words before, 'and only in the kitchen because it's just us three.'

Only the kitchen was as big as the whole of the ground floor of the Banana House, and a place of shining steel and immaculate tiles, nothing at all like the Casson kitchen. Pot luck turned out to be baked cheese soufflé, salad and hot rolls, and pineapple pudding with home-made ice cream. No trace of a pot in sight, Saffron noticed, nor, for that matter, of any other cooking utensil. The whole meal seemed to have appeared as if by magic on the huge pine table, complete with linen napkins, sparkling spring water for the girls and wine for Mrs Warbeck.

With the food went polite conversation. Mrs Warbeck led this, tactfully avoiding the subject of school and sticking to holidays. Foreign holidays in particular. This limited Saffron to her school trip to Boulogne with the French class just before Christmas,

69

the only foreign holiday she had ever had. Unfortunately there was not much about the Boulogne trip that could be comfortably explained to the headmistress of the private school.

'Did you enjoy the shops?' enquired Sarah's mother and Saffron said yes, she had enjoyed the shops until some people had been caught shoplifting.

'Not me!' she added hastily, and Sarah's mother said no, no, of course, not you, but it killed the conversation a bit.

'I,' said Sarah, startlingly, 'should like to go to Italy. Siena.'

Saffron, forgetting Sarah had bad legs, kicked her hard under the table.

'Siena,' said Sarah, not flinching at all. 'Couldn't we? Couldn't we? Couldn't we?'

'Sarah, darling!'

'Because I long and long and long to go to Siena,' said Sarah. 'Couldn't we, one weekend?'

'Don't be silly, Sarah!'

Sarah hung her head.

Saffron glared. While she glared a large tear, a real tear, rolled down Sarah's cheek and splashed on the table. Followed by another. Saffron had never seen anything like it. All at once she began to understand how so much stuff had accumulated in Sarah's bedroom.

'Sarah darling, it would be a long, long trip! A holiday sort of trip, not something we could do in a weekend! Anyway, why Siena?'

'I heard about a garden in Siena,' said Sarah. 'A little white stone garden, with water in it, and dark pointed trees . . .'

'I expect there are lots of gardens like that in Siena,' said her mother, smiling.

Sarah nodded and picked up her water glass and took a sip. The glass trembled a little against her teeth. 'There was an angel in the garden,' she said.

'An angel?' repeated her mother.

'A stone angel,' said Sarah.

Saffron stared at her, absolutely outraged, and Sarah gave her a brief, triumphant glance, from tear-sparkling eyes.

'Where did you hear about this beautiful garden?' asked Sarah's mother.

'From a girl,' said Sarah unblushingly. 'Could we go to Siena for my birthday present? If I never had another present, ever, ever, ever?'

'I can't just say yes, Sarah! Without even speaking to your father! What do you think about all this, Saffron?'

'I don't think she should go to Siena!' burst out Saffron. 'I don't think you should let her! Just because she suddenly wants to! Just like that! Why should she?'

'Why shouldn't she?' asked Sarah's mother, quite startled at Saffron's fury.

Saffron wanted to shout, Because it is mine! My Siena! My garden! My angel! Sarah has enough already! She has a room full of stuff!

None of these answers were possible of course. They were all too close to the words Rich Kids'

School, Jealous, and Spoilt Only Child. They were too bad.

Saffron, trying to avoid them, said something infinitely worse.

'Because she's got bad legs!'

The moment she had said it she knew it was wrong. Sarah, all traces of tears now vanished, glanced at her in delight. Sarah's mother said,

'Yes, Saffron, it is true that Sarah's legs are not so strong as yours. You are quite right to think about that. But so far they have not stopped her doing anything that she really wants do. *Anything!*' she repeated with such great emphasis that Saffron half expected her to add, 'So There!'

How wrong you are! thought Saffron, remembering Sarah's talk the previous day of bikes and skateboards and roller blades. It was no good saying so though. She had said too much already.

'I've got to go home now,' she muttered miserably. 'Thank you for tea. Supper.'

'It was very nice to have you,' said Sarah's mother. 'You must come again. Sarah will go with you to the door.'

Sarah moved awkwardly after sitting so long, clumsily, like a mermaid on rocks. She seemed to feel awkward too, because at the front door she touched Saffron's arm and said, 'Sorry I made you mad, Saff!'

'Huh,' said Saffron.

'Don't quarrel! Don't let's fight!'

'Spoilt only child!'

'Jealous!'

'Rich kids' school!'

After that they both felt better.

'Look,' said Sarah. 'I'm going to Siena! I bet I'm going to Siena!'

'I bet you are too!'

'You give me the address of the house where you used to live, and I'll go there!'

'Go to my house!'

'I could find out what happened to your angel!'

'*I'll* go to my house,' said Saffron furiously, 'and find out what happened to my angel! Not you!'

Chapter Six

A most unexpected thing happened at the Banana House. Rose received a cheque, one hundred and forty-four pounds, proving that her grandfather's will had not been nothing more than kind thoughts after all. It was presented to her by her mother one Sunday afternoon, always the Casson time for important events.

'It will just about buy you another party dress,' said Bill, who had never recovered from the extravagance of the last one.

A cheque meant nothing at all to Rose. She read her name on it and asked, 'Is that me?'

'Of course it is,' said her father, laughing at her puzzled face.

The cheque was pale blue and looked to Rose like a label. Saffron and Caddy and Indigo all came to inspect it, and seeing it made them feel solemn.

Caddy said, 'I wonder what happened to Indigo's car?'

'Dropped to bits,' answered her father. 'Years ago.'

'And my house?'

'Probably over the cliff by now.'

'And Saffy's angel?'

The last thing Bill Casson wanted was another Sunday afternoon row about Saffy's angel. He said, 'My taxi will be here any minute!' and disappeared upstairs for his bag.

Rose did not have a bank account, but Caddy did. She paid Rose's cheque into it, and immediately took it out again in the form of one hundred and forty-four one pound coins. Then Rose was really pleased with her inheritance. She played with the coins for several days, sorting and stacking them on the kitchen table.

'What are you going to do with them all?' asked Indigo.

Rose arranged them into a three-dimensional dragon hoard on thick black card, glued them together, and with Caddy's help, sprayed the whole lot gold.

'I bet you don't send that to me in London!' said her father the next time he came home. He had been quite nice about Rose's jammy picture. It was just bad luck that he had mistaken it for food supplies from Eve, instead of art from Rose, and had consequently dropped it in the bin.

'Whenever have I ever sent you food supplies?' demanded Eve, and Bill reminded her of the time she had posted him a home-made sponge birthday cake, labelled hopefully but futilely: FRAGILE and THIS WAY UP.

Another unexpected thing that happened was

Michael announcing it was about time Caddy applied for her driving test.

'But I asked you not long ago if I should, and you just laughed!' said Caddy.

'Times change,' said Michael. 'There's a written test first, and then the exam.'

'I suppose Diane passed first time?'

'Obviously.'

'It's all exams,' said Caddy sighing. 'Do you know what is in June? All my resits. Five GCSEs and three A levels.'

'About time too,' said Michael, but added mercifully, 'That's all Diane did, three A levels. You'll cope, easy!'

Caddy felt unreasonably cheered by this opinion. For several weeks now she had been working very hard, and it was nice to hear she was catching up with Diane a little bit.

'How old is she?' she asked.

'Diane,' said Michael. 'Forty-five.'

'*Forty-five!*'

'If a day,' said Michael. 'There, that was very good! If I'd told you that three weeks ago you'd have done an emergency stop and burst into tears! She's twenty-one.'

Caddy sighed because twenty-one was obviously the perfect age for Droopy Di.

'We'll go and practise parking in very small spaces,' said Michael. 'That'll cheer you up! And you can tell me all about the kids at home. Has your brother fallen

76

out of the window yet?'

'No,' replied Caddy. 'Although I think it is just a matter of time. He has been making something in his bedroom which he says will help him. He makes Rose guard the door while he is doing it. Rose is a very good guard.'

'If he wants I'll sign him in at the gym and start him off on the climbing wall. I'm going tonight. Would your mother let him come?'

'Michael darling,' said Caddy, brightening up at once. '*I* will come with you to the gym! You can start *me* off on the climbing wall! You can teach me and I can teach Indigo!'

'Don't call me darling, I'm a driving instructor,' replied Michael automatically. 'No thank you, Cadmium dear! Teaching you to drive is more than enough. I go to the gym to relax.'

'Oh well,' said Caddy. 'It was worth a try. And actually I told Indigo what you said about the climbing wall in the gym, and he said it would not be scary enough. It's got to be really scary, he says, otherwise there's no point. This is a smart road! What are we doing here?'

Michael said they were looking for a gap to park in, and presently he found one, in behind a white Mercedes and in front of an open-topped Lotus. He ordered Caddy to park in the space between them without touching either.

'I can't I can't I can't,' said Caddy. 'I'd never park in a place like that in real life.'

'You can if you just relax,' said Michael. 'Go on to automatic pilot. Tell me what your mother thinks of all this scary stuff on the windowsill. Doesn't she worry?'

'I don't know,' said Caddy as she reversed nervously past the Mercedes. 'He mostly does it when she's out. Painting or teaching. Old ladies today. In a home. She makes them paint. Am I too close?'

'No. You're fine. What do the old ladies paint?'

'Pictures of their past. In acrylic colours, so it all looks much brighter than it really was. It's good for them, she says.'

'Very nice of her.'

'She gets paid,' said Caddy. 'That's why she does it. Not to be nice. Actually the old ladies don't like it much at all. They moan, but they still keep coming ... There! I'm in!'

'Brilliant! Told you you could do it!'

'Michael darling?'

'Um?'

'If I pass this driving test . . .'

'When, not if!'

'. . . Won't you miss me?'

'You forget,' said Michael. 'I have Diane. The gorgeous.'

'Oh yes.'

'And intelligent.'

'Yes.'

'Extremely well qualified and rodent free.'

'Yes, yes.'

'Aged twenty-one. The perfect age.'

'Tattooed?' asked Caddy.

'Heavily,' said Michael enthusiastically.

'My sister Saffron has just got a nose stud. Gold.'

'Diane has several. Diamond.'

'It always sounds so painful.'

'Diane is very brave. Holes everywhere.'

'Like a sieve?'

'A human colander,' agreed Michael.

They arrived home again to a most peculiar sight. The small garden at the front of the Banana House had been transformed. A tidal wave of cushions, bean bags, quilts, hearth rugs, and sleeping bags appeared to have swept up the lawn and broken at the wall. From Indigo's window a multicoloured rope of knotted bed sheets came snaking out and ended among the cushions. As Michael and Caddy watched, a mattress emerged and fell to the ground, followed a moment later by a rain of pillows.

'Indigo!' shouted Caddy, jumping out of the car.

Indigo and Rose's heads appeared in the window above.

'It's all right, Caddy!' Indigo called cheerfully. 'We've been doing it all the time you've been gone.'

'We keep finding more stuff to land on!' added Rose. 'Look!'

She stepped aside to make room for Indigo, who, ignoring Caddy's screams, climbed casually on to the windowsill, rolled over on to his front and slid down the multicoloured snake on to the sea of cushions. Rose followed after, landing with a bounce on the mattress. There she continued to bounce up and down while explaining that the whole arrangement was perfectly safe and that the other end of the rope was being looked after by Saffron, who had tied it to the bed leg, and was guarding the knot.

'What stupid, stupid kids!' exclaimed Michael.

Indigo and Rose stopped bouncing and stared at him in astonishment. Saffron appeared at the window above and glared scornfully down.

'Who,' said Rose, 'asked you?'

'He doesn't mean to be rude,' said Caddy apologetically. 'He likes to be safe. And it does look highly dangerous!'

'I bet your mother doesn't know what you're up to!' said Michael.

'She does!' said Indigo triumphantly. 'Rose told her!'

'What, and she said you could?' asked Michael in disbelief.

'She said "Enjoy yourselves, chickens, and don't let go of the rope",' said Rose. 'So there! Are you another of Caddy's boyfriends?'

'No,' said Michael crossly, while Indigo and Saffron both loudly explained to Rose that Michael was much too old to be anyone's boyfriend. 'No, I'm not! I'm a driving instructor!'

'How twitchy he is!' remarked Saffron as Michael drove away.

80

'Not always,' said Caddy loyally. 'Do you really think it's safe to help Indigo and Rose climb out of that window?'

'Of course it's not safe,' said Saffron. 'But they'd do it anyway, and it's safer if I help. Did you come past Sarah's house?'

'Yes, and I remembered to look, and her mother's car is there outside.'

Saffron sighed.

'It's a lovely nose stud,' said Caddy comfortingly, collecting up cushions. 'It looks fantastic. So did Sarah's! I don't know what's the matter with Sarah's mother.'

'Says it's common,' said Saffron gloomily. 'Rude old bat! And she said perhaps we'd been seeing a bit too much of each other and Sarah needed time to concentrate on her school work more.'

'She'll soon forget.'

'Caddy,' said Saffron impatiently, 'she is headmistress of the private school! She's probably never forgotten anything in her whole life!'

'You ought to tell her it was Sarah's idea!'

'Sarah told her.'

'What did she say?'

'She said, "Really Sarah, you never thought of such a thing until Saffron came on the scene"!'

'She is a rude old bat then,' agreed Caddy.

When Saffron had returned from town on Saturday with a nose stud, nobody at the Banana House had been rude.

'Sweet, Saffy darling! Clever you!' said Eve.

'I want one,' said Rose.

'I want an earring,' said Indigo. 'If it doesn't hurt.'

'It hurts,' said Saffron, not wanting to be upstaged by Indigo and an earring.

'Even Dad likes it,' remarked Caddy, and her father agreed that he did. In a way. Being a broadminded, tolerant, artistic sort of person. Or so people told him . . .

'Oh yes?' said Saffron, rolling her eyes.

'Yes,' said Bill, sounding a little bit peeved. 'So you thank your lucky stars my girl, because in some families you would have come home to very big trouble! A nose stud! At your age! If you come down with blood poisoning don't blame me!'

At Sarah's house her mother was saying much the same thing, and since nobody had ever accused her of being broadminded or tolerant or artistic she was saying it very plainly indeed, and a lot of other things too, all of them about Saffron and none of them complimentary.

This was a great shame because things had been going very well between Saffron and Sarah until the nose stud afternoon.

Sarah's mother had become quite used to seeing Saffron around the house. At first she had been concerned that they seemed to spend almost all their time arguing, but after a while she had decided that it was a good sort of arguing. She was always so terribly afraid that people would patronise Sarah. Saffron certainly did not do that. Also, in a clumsy but well meaning kind of way she tried to look after her a bit.

Mrs Warbeck began to think she might be a suitable friend for Sarah after all. The day that Saffron, trying out the racing wheelchair for the first time, took a chunk out of the bottom of the banisters and sent a stand of plants crashing to the floor in the hall, she found herself quite liking her.

'I'm sorry, I'm sorry!' wailed Saffron, kneeling in a sea of potting compost and scrabbling up crushed geraniums from the floor. 'Shut up laughing, Sarah! It's not funny!'

Sarah was sitting on the bottom stair, howling with laughter.

'Take no notice!' said her mother, bending down to help Saffron. 'I should think it is at least half Sarah's fault. If not more. And don't worry about the flowers. They were getting far too leggy. And it was only an old pot . . . Are you crying, Saffron?'

'No.'

'It's horrible smashing things in other people's houses.'

'I never cry.'

'I once broke a mirror at a friend's. Seven years' bad luck.'

'Who got the bad luck, you or your friend?'

'She did. Fetch a brush, Sarah, don't just sit there watching! Did you hear we were going to Italy, Saffron?'

'Yes.'

Siena was now an accepted fact. Sarah was going at half term and she had managed her parents so well that they half thought the whole idea had been theirs from the start. The journey had been planned, the hotel booked and it was just a matter of whether or not to invite Saffron to go with them.

'I'm going one day,' volunteered Saffron, as she brushed up spilt compost.

'To Italy?'

'To Siena,' said Saffron.

Mrs Warbeck very nearly did invite her then. The only thing that stopped her was the thought of how disappointed she and Sarah would be if Mr and Mrs Casson should say no. She thought she would talk to them first, and meanwhile she offered to drive both girls into town the next day, which was a Saturday. She would drop them off together, Sarah and Saffron and the wheelchair, to do as they liked for the afternoon. There was the cinema, she said, and shops, and a lovely friendly restaurant in the basement of the library, and Sarah could take her mobile phone and call whenever they wanted to come home. Saffron was flattered to be so trusted, and Sarah, who had never in her whole life been allowed into town on her own, was astonished and delighted.

At first it went very well. They started with the cinema and went on to the shops. They skipped the friendly restaurant in favour of pizza slices and chips in the town square, and it was while they were eating these that a group of girls from Saffron's school turned up and demanded to know what Saffron was doing with a girl from the rich kids' school. They all had brand new nose studs.

'Mind your own business,' said Saffron defensively. 'She can't help being a private school kid. She has to go there. Her mother's the head.'

'Shut up, Saffron!' said Sarah laughing, and then she turned to the girls and asked, 'Where did you get your noses done?'

This question changed the atmosphere completely. The girls crowded round to explain how noses were being done that day in a very sterile van at the back of the market. Solid gold studs, said the girls proudly, six pounds a time, a never to be repeated bargain. Saffron, who was listening with growing alarm, was very relieved to hear that the girls had got their nose studs only just in time, the van was packing up right now, and the woman in charge had remarked only a few minutes earlier that she was about done for the day.

'Oh no, she isn't!' exclaimed Sarah. 'They look absolutely brilliant! I'm having one too!'

Then to Saffron's horror she set off at top speed for the back of the market, causing great trouble among the stalls with her wheelchair. All the girls from Saffron's school, and Saffron too, ran after her reminding her that nose studs were banned at her school, as were dangling earrings, hair extensions, trainers, mobile phones and many, many other things loathed by Sarah's mother.

'Who cares?' asked Sarah cheerfully, and to Saffron she said, 'You're scared.'

This meant Saffron had to have a nose stud too, and during the process (at which Sarah did not flinch) she went sick and grey and dizzy. The owner of the mobile nose stud van, who had seen it all before, callously drove off.

'Never mind,' said Sarah. 'I'll ring my mother.'

Sarah's mother (who had been waiting by the phone all afternoon) arrived very promptly. She found Sarah and Saffron sitting among the litter of the market, surrounded by a gang of girls all equipped with dangling earrings, trainers, mobile phones and nose studs. At the sight of the private school head they melted away like snow in summer with calls of, 'See you Monday, Saff!'

'Get in the car!' said Sarah's mother, purple with fury, but determined not to make a scene in public. 'Get in the car and we will talk about this on the way home.'

Saffron had been dropped off at the Banana House in disgrace.

Since then she had not seen Sarah once, although Sarah had telephoned and said how sorry she was. She had told Saffron how nearly she had been invited to Siena. She had promised to explain everything to her mother and get Saffron there yet, as soon as her mother would calm down and listen to explanations. If Saffron would just find out the address in Siena of the place where she used to live, said Sarah, she would bring home her stone angel herself, single handed if necessary.

'No,' said Saffron. 'It's my angel. I'll get it myself.'

'It's only a few weeks till half term,' said Sarah. 'My mother might not come round before then. She is very mad.'

'Whose fault is that?' demanded Saffron, and Sarah admitted at once that it was hers.

'I didn't ask,' said Saffron (shouted actually), 'for you to stick your nose in my business! Or for you to get me to Siena! Or for your mother to go taking me into town! I can go into town whenever I like!'

'I know, I know,' said Sarah meekly.

'Or for this rotten nose stud! You made me!'

'You like it though.'

'I nearly died!'

'Yes, but you like it now.'

'That's not the point!'

'Saffron, please say you like it otherwise I'll have got a hole in your nose for nothing.'

'Yes, all right. I do. Quite.'

'I knew you did. Saffron. I've got another plan. I'm working on it. I'll ring you when it's perfect . . . Here's my mother coming! Should you like to talk to Saffron, Mummy dear?'

'No,' said Saffron in panic. 'Don't let her!'

'It's quite funny,' said Sarah, in a loud, conversational voice. 'Because of nose studs being banned at the rich kids' school, you know? I've had a Head's warning! I may have to come to the comprehensive . . . There, she's stamped off! Don't worry, Saffron! Wait till you've heard my plan!'

Chapter Seven

Caddy was in the front room, crouched on the carpet, laying out around her a complicated pattern of papers and books and files.

'Now, don't move anything!' she said to Indigo, who was watching. 'I have arranged them all in the order that I'm supposed to learn them. If I start at the sofa and work my way over to the window I shall know it all!'

'What a brilliant idea!' said Indigo.

'People will just have to step over it all until after the exams.'

'What is it?'

'Economics.'

'What's that stuff in your bedroom then? Rose was showing me. Sellotaped all over the ceiling.'

'Biology. I'm putting a different subject in every room. Chemistry in the kitchen, with fridge magnets and blutack. French in the bathroom upstairs so I can write vocab. on the tiles and learn it in the bath. English literature will be fine in the downstairs loo, because it's just reading. Physics I do at college because I've got a friend there who is very good at it, and you can't revise English language. It's instinct, English language. I only failed it before because I turned over two pages of the exam paper at once and missed out all the middle questions.'

'What about maths?' asked Indigo, who had been keeping track of all this on his fingers.

Caddy, who detested maths, pretended not to hear.

'*What* about maths?' repeated Indigo.

'Maths is instinct too,' said Caddy rather defensively. 'Anyway, what does it matter? I expect I shall fail everything again, just like last time.'

Indigo looked at her in astonishment.

' 'Course you won't fail everything!' he said. 'How can you go to university and do zoology if you fail everything? Don't you want to do that any more?'

'Of course I do.'

'You were going to work in a game reserve in Africa and have me over for holidays to get warmed up from my polar expeditions!'

This was a plan they had made together years ago, the Christmas they had both had chicken pox. Their father had come home from London and put them both into isolation upstairs, so that Rose should not be infected. They had been there for nearly two weeks, watching the rain fall past the bedroom window, and Caddy had longed for sunshine, and Indigo had longed for snow, and together they had planned out futures in lands where the weather was more enjoyable. Caddy had forgotten all about it, but Indigo, who never forgot anything, had been looking forward to his holidays in Africa with Caddy for years.

'Can't we still do it?' he asked.

'I wish we could.'

'This time,' said Indigo, 'you won't fail anything. *I* don't believe you did last time! I think they just got the marking wrong!'

'Oh, Indigo!'

'And look how hard you're working now!'

Caddy groaned.

'You can put your maths in my bedroom if you like. Because I don't think it is instinct. So that can be your maths place.'

'Indigo,' said Caddy. 'Do you truly think I will pass all these exams and go to university and study zoology and end up working on a game reserve?'

'Yes,' said Indigo.

'And pass my driving test as well?'

'Yes, of course,' said Indigo, slightly surprised that Caddy, the eldest and cleverest, and most beautiful member of his pack, should have so many doubts. 'And I've been thinking if you didn't mind working in Australia instead of Africa it would be much handier for the South Pole. Only I know there's terrible crocodiles.'

'Crocodiles,' said Caddy, as she bent over the start of the economics trail to begin her revision, 'wouldn't bother me at all!'

'I didn't think they would,' said Indigo.

★　　★　　★

A week or two later Sarah telephoned Saffron with details of her plan (now perfect). It was that Saffron should become a stowaway.

'A what?' shouted Saffron.

'A stowaway,' said Sarah.

It was so simple, she explained. Saffron needed to go to Siena, and why should she not? Stowing away would be the easiest thing in the world. There would be plenty of space in the car. It was simply a matter of Saffron remaining concealed on the back seat until Sarah's parents had driven to the point of no return.

'Probably the ferry,' said Sarah. 'But the further the better of course.'

Then all Saffron would have to do (said Sarah) was emerge from her hiding place, and explain politely that here she was, after all. At which Sarah's parents would probably reply, well, well, so she was, what an excellent surprise. Something like that, anyway. And Saffron must be sure to remember her passport and some money (in case as a last resort they had to actually buy the angel) (Don't be silly, Saffron, English money will be fine! They'll change it at the hotel for you!) and the address of her old home in Siena. Also she should leave a letter explaining where she was so that her family need not be worried.

'I have thought of everything,' said Sarah complacently, and went on to describe how Saffron's clothes could be smuggled down the road to the Warbecks' house and packed among Sarah's own where they would not be noticed.

'I will say I want to take my bean bag,' said Sarah, ignoring Saffron's squeaks down the phone. 'I often take my bean bag on car trips. It's enormous, and you're not very big. I'll empty it out and cover you in the cover and pile a lot of stuff around and they'll never notice. They're used to me having a lot of stuff. As you know. What do you say?'

'Goodbye,' said Saffron. 'You have obviously gone mad.'

'Get everything you want to bring with you sorted out right now and I will telephone you when it is safe to bring it down. This evening probably. The sooner the better.'

'Bonkers,' said Saffron, beginning to laugh. 'Totally cracked. You are falling apart. I suppose I will get the blame for that too.'

'Don't bother with a hair dryer, you can share mine.'

'I haven't got a hair dryer. I have drip-dry hair. I am not a Private School Kid.'

'Saffron, it will be fun! An adventure. And perhaps we'll find your angel. It was there, wasn't it? In the garden? In Siena?'

Saffron did not say anything.

'Pack!' said Sarah. 'Do it now!'

Still Saffron did not reply.

'Obviously,' snapped Sarah, 'you are scared of my mother.'

'*Obviously* I am scared of your mother!' said Saffron. '*And* your dad!'

'Dad's a pussy cat,' said Sarah soothingly. 'You wait and see! And Mum just pretends to be tough. It's her job. She's not really scary at all. Nothing compared to me!'

'I never said she was,' said Saffron crossly, putting down the phone.

She turned round, and there were Caddy, Indigo and Rose, all shamelessly listening to her half of the conversation and eager to hear more.

'Why did you say you were scared of Sarah's parents?' demanded Indigo.

'Why were you laughing?' asked Caddy. 'Why did you say she'd gone mad?'

'What did she want?' asked Rose, coming sensibly to the point.

Saffron explained that Sarah had arranged for her to stow away in the family car to Italy, in order to hunt out the stone angel that had been left to her in their grandfather's will.

She waited for them to gasp with disbelief, and to agree that Sarah must indeed be quite mad, bonkers, cracked and falling apart.

'Absolutely fantastic,' said Caddy. 'Totally completely what you ought to do! Darling Mum will never agree of course, but I will cover for you until you get away.'

'You're not really scared of Sarah's parents, are you?' asked Indigo. 'I didn't think you were scared of anything.'

'When are you going?' asked Rose.

Then all together they talked about how lucky Saffron was to have a friend like Sarah, and how much they wished that they could go too. Caddy found Eve's address book and turned back the pages until she came to *Linda, 16 Via S. Francesco, Siena.*

It was the last of a whole page of Linda addresses; there was *Linda, Rome, Linda, Cambridge*, and *Linda, London*. They had all been crossed out except the last.

It startled them to see that last address still waiting on the page.

'As if she was still there,' said Caddy.

'That was where you lived,' said Indigo, and Saffron thought, Yes, that was where I lived.

Just to see it written down was astonishing.

Caddy began to talk about the time that followed the death of Saffron's mother.

'Grandad brought you to us,' she said. 'In his big green car, his Bentley. I can remember that. It was full of your toys and clothes and things. And you were crying. And Mum was crying. And me and Indigo were crying and Dad kept trying to make everyone be sensible.'

Saffron could picture that very easily indeed.

'Dad is very bossy,' observed Rose. 'And he is always trying to make other people be sensible but he doesn't know what sensible is. That's why he lives in London and paints rubbish pictures!'

Caddy ignored all this and carried on.

'Everyone was fussing around you. Grandad said you'd had to leave something behind and he ought to

95

have brought it for you, that's what you were crying about. He said he felt like turning right round and going back to fetch it. Dad said Grandad was being ridiculous and everyone should go to bed. I remember it was all very noisy and miserable and Grandad got mad with Dad and wouldn't stay. He unloaded the car and went. But he said goodbye to me first.'

'What did he say?' asked Saffron.

'He said, "Don't cry, Caddy. Everything will be all right in the morning." I remember that because later on Mum was looking after you, and Dad took me and Indigo up to bed. I was still sniffing a bit and Dad said, "Don't cry, Caddy, everything will be all right in the morning." Exactly the same.

'We didn't see Grandad again for a long time and when we did he was not the same person. He didn't look the same, and he didn't speak. But I didn't know exactly what had happened to him for ages and ages. Not until I was nearly grown up.'

'What happened to him?' demanded Saffy.

'He got very ill,' said Caddy. 'He had a heart attack, driving. In Southampton. A week or two after he brought you home. He was on his way back to Siena. He must have been. Mum and Dad guessed that. And now we know he must have been going to get your angel. He would have got it for you if he could, Saffy.'

'I know.'

'I'm so glad you are going. I'll help you pack!'

'Pack!' repeated Saffron. She had completely forgotten Sarah's terrible plan while she listened to

Caddy's story, and it was a bit of a jolt to come back into the present.

'You can borrow any of my things you like!'

'Or mine,' said Indigo. 'You can borrow my new sports bag. You will need to take something strong to carry it back. Stone's heavy.'

'But it might not even be there!'

'Where else would it be?'

'And that place in the address book will be someone else's house now. And someone else's garden. And perhaps their angel.'

'It can't be anyone's angel except yours,' said Rose.

'Think about it, Saffy!' said Caddy. 'Think! A chance to go back!'

Saffron looked again at the last uncrossed out address in the address book and thought about it. The place that she had remembered in so many dreams, the garden with the white stone paths and the high walls and the little pointed trees, was there.

'Sarah said bring money,' she remembered suddenly. 'In case we have to buy it. I haven't got any money.'

Caddy turned at once to the housekeeping jar and Indigo pointed out that Rose had stacks of money.

'I do?' said Rose, surprised.

Indigo reminded her that she still had her inheritance, one hundred and forty-four pounds.

Rose said at once that the one hundred and forty-four pounds was no longer money, but art, and anyway all glued down.

'*And* sprayed gold,' she added unhelpfully.

'Rose!' whispered Indigo indignantly.

'I don't want Rose's money!' said Saffron. 'And I don't want that either!' she added, as Caddy emptied the contents of the housekeeping jam jar out on to the kitchen table. 'I don't want to go at all!'

Rose, who was quite aware that she was not coming up to the very high standards of behaviour that Indigo expected of his pack, decided to get away from the kitchen while no one was taking any notice of her. Just as she was going out of the door, however, the telephone rang. She picked it up, listened for a moment without saying a word, and then passed it across to Saffron.

'Sarah!' said Saffron, with a groan in her voice.

Rose paused in the doorway. Sarah's voice, very high and excited, was clear to everyone in the room.

'Did you sort out your stuff?' she demanded. 'You could come over right now! She's just gone out. I found a little job for her. And brilliant news, Saffy, she says it's too late to change the hotel booking! She'd got me a room with two beds in case you came, and booked for four of us on the ferry. She's been trying to make me choose someone from school to ask . . . did you pack?'

'No, I . . .'

'Well, go and do it! I thought you'd have finished! Do it straight away!'

'You are so bossy!'

'Oh, Saffron!' wailed Sarah down the phone. 'I'm

not bossy! I'm *helping* you! I'm very, very efficient! Now, quick, go and get your stuff!'

A whirlwind of activity suddenly began around Saffron. Rose had a change of heart, fetched her golden dragon hoard from the windowsill and began levering off the first coins. Caddy hurried upstairs, and reappeared carrying her own new white jeans and her black denim jacket. Indigo emptied his football kit out of his sports bag and handed it over to Caddy.

'Five minutes!' he told Sarah, taking the receiver out of Saffron's hand. 'Don't worry! She'll be there in five minutes!'

'No, I won't!' shouted Saffron, grabbing it back. 'You know I can't!'

'Five minutes absolute max!' said Sarah autocratically, and put down the phone.

Five minutes later, with the sports bag full, Saffron was pushed out of the front door by everyone in the house.

'Hurry back!' said Indigo. 'We've still got all Rose's money to scrub clean!'

'Ask Sarah if she knows what gets off Super Glue!' said Caddy.

'Run!' ordered Rose, and Saffy found herself running down the road to Sarah's house.

Sarah was waiting by her open front door and she pounced on Saffron at once.

'I can hardly wait until half term!' she exclaimed, her face alight with plotting. 'You'll have to go in a minute though, Saffy, before my mother comes back.

It took me ages to think of a job for her. She's gone over to school to fetch my Latin book.'

'Latin!'

'Oh yes,' said Sarah airily. 'All private school kids do Latin. It is ancient Italian. It'll be useful, you'll see! Now, listen! I'm working on how to actually get you into the car. On the day. I'll let you know. I'll think of another job for my mother and telephone again!'

'You're enjoying all this!'

'Yes,' said Sarah, making her wheelchair spin round very fast backwards and then forwards again. 'Just call me Mission Control! Any questions?'

'Caddy said ask you what gets Super Glue off.'

'Nothing, I don't think. Why?'

'Tell you another time.'

'You'd better go now Saffy, you really had.'

'All right. Shall I take my bag up to your room?'

'I'll do it.'

'I'll be much faster,' said Saffron, and ran upstairs with it before Sarah could argue any more. 'Sorry,' she said seeing Sarah's face as she came back down.

'Doesn't matter,' growled Sarah, and then she said suddenly, 'I do miss you,' and rubbed the studless side of her nose.

'So do I,' said Saffron, quite touched. 'Miss you, I mean. Bye bye, Mission Control!'

'Bye, Super Hero!' said Sarah.

Chapter Eight

Caddy's exams were spread out over a whole month, the week before the summer half term holiday at the end of May, and the two weeks after it. Before they started she had the written part of her driving test, which she passed with no trouble at all.

'Told you so!' said Michael.

Caddy hardly noticed she had done it. She had begun to spend her time in a trance of exam papers and revision, trekking from room to room in the Banana House in search of ever more knowledge. It became a sort of safari. She hunted down facts and theories, and was mildly astonished to find that once she had found them they stayed in her brain.

Occasionally the safari was not successful and she stuck in a bog. English literature was a terrible bog, especially Shakespeare, especially, especially *Hamlet*, the play. For three years Caddy had owned a copy of *Hamlet*. Somehow, she could not read it. It numbed her brain. She still had not got through it the day before the English literature exam.

'I will just have to skip all the Shakespeare questions,' she told Indigo.

'Like you did last time?'

'Um. Yes.'

'You'd better read it,' said Indigo.

'There isn't time. I've got a driving lesson.'

'Cancel it,' said Indigo austerely.

Caddy rang up Michael.

'I have to read this totally boring play,' she explained. '*Hamlet*. By Shakespeare. Droopy Di probably loves it.'

'You are quite right,' agreed Michael cordially. 'Shakespeare. Oh yes. Reads it in the bath.'

'How do you know? No, don't tell me! Anyway, Michael darling, because of this terrible *Hamlet* that I have to know all about before tomorrow I'm afraid I won't be able to come out with you today.'

'Who was he, then?' asked Michael. 'I think I have a right to know. Since you are cancelling at such short notice, Cadmium dear!'

'He was a Prince,' said Caddy. 'Of Denmark.'

'I've been there,' said Michael, sounding very pleased with himself. 'I went to a concert in Denmark, years ago! In a sea of mud. Never stopped raining for three days. Terrible place, Denmark!'

'Hamlet went mad.'

'So did a lot of us.'

'And his girlfriend drowned.'

'Not surprised at all. Wettest place I've ever seen.'

'She was called Ophelia.'

'And she couldn't swim?'

'No.'

'Poor old Oph.'

'Yes,' agreed Caddy, beginning to feel a bit better, 'and poor old Ham, in all that mud.'

'Think of me, when you read it,' said Michael. 'My tent was pinched and my two best mates got food poisoning.'

'Hamlet's two best mates got murdered.'

'Dear, oh dear,' said Michael. 'I'll see you next week then.'

That got Caddy out of the *Hamlet* bog quite nicely. She substituted Michael for Hamlet, and herself for Ophelia, and she added the two best mates whenever the action got very slow, and somehow she got through the whole play in time to discuss it, quite intelligently, in the examination the next day. Still, it was a great relief to go back to Chemistry, which was written in plain English and full of familiar names from the colour chart, still pinned on the kitchen wall.

'You are working too hard,' remarked Eve, coming in from an afternoon with the local Young Offenders, whom she had recently been employed to turn into Young Artists instead. 'I never did any work at all when I was your age!'

'What *did* you do?' enquired Rose.

'I had a lovely time! I was a hippy!'

'I bet Dad wasn't!' said Rose.

'Don't worry about Caddy,' Indigo told his mother. 'I am keeping her strength up with high energy food. Raisins and biscuits and corned beef for pemmican. Like the explorers had at the South Pole.'

'They ate their dogs too,' remarked Rose. 'You told me. Is Caddy having dog?'

'Captain Scott didn't eat his dogs,' said Indigo crossly.

'But,' pointed out Rose, who was in a rather awkward mood that evening, 'he died. So!'

Eve said that what Caddy needed was not raisins or biscuits or corned beef or dog, but a nice evening out with her friends, relaxing. She picked up Caddy's chemistry notes and said she did not see how Caddy could possibly be expected to understand any of it.

'Even my Young Offenders would make nothing of it,' she said, 'and they are quite extraordinarily bright. This afternoon one of them showed me how to unlock my car with a teaspoon and a freezer bag tie. He did it in seconds! I'd never have got home if he hadn't. I'd locked my keys inside. Anyway, Indigo needn't cook dog tonight. I was going to make everyone pancakes. What do you think?'

'Lovely!'

'Where's Saffron?'

Saffron was upstairs, wondering for the fiftieth time at least, if it was worth all the trouble of stowing away to Italy to find a stone angel that she had seen last when she was three years old. Once again she unfolded the little piece of paper that had been fastened to her grandfather's will.

For Saffron. Her angel in the garden. The stone angel.

The following Monday, having somehow survived the first week of exams, Caddy stuck her head through Michael's car window and said, 'Michael darling!'

'*Don't* call me that!'

'I can't come for this driving lesson unless you do me a huge enormous favour, which I know you will.'

Michael screwed his eyes tight shut and waited.

'Let me bring . . .'

'No, no, no!' shouted Michael. '*Please* no more livestock!'

'They're not livestock! They will be no trouble at all.'

'Hamsters, guinea pigs, what next?'

'Only Indigo and Rose.'

'Oh, come on, Caddy!' exploded Michael. 'Have a heart! This is a driving lesson. Not Fun at the Zoo. Not Babysitters on Wheels!'

'I can't come then,' said Caddy. 'I promised I'd look after them. I was sure you wouldn't mind.'

'Why aren't they at school?'

'It's half term.'

'Why can't your mother look after them?'

'She's working. She's started teaching a crash course for Young Offenders. It's called Art for Art's Sake. They're all very clever and they've taught her how to break into cars. Didn't Darling Diane ever bring her little brothers and sisters with her on driving lessons?'

'Nope.'

'Oh. All right then. Bye, bye Michael.'

'Yes. OK. If they must I suppose I can stick it,'

groaned Michael, breaking down under this enormous pressure.

'You *are* a darling, Michael,' said Caddy, and turned and waved at the blank windows of the house. Indigo and Rose immediately appeared, both beaming cheerfully and looking not at all surprised.

'Tricked,' said Michael, as they scrambled into the back seat. 'Conned, stitched up and taken for a ride! Mind, not a squeak out of either of you, however she drives. Grin and bear it like I have to. Now then Cadmium, start the engine. Mirror, signal . . .'

'I know all that now, Michael darling.'

'Just reminding you. I thought there were three of them.'

'Three of what?' asked Caddy.

'Haven't you got another sister?'

'Oh yes, Saffron,' said Caddy.

'Saffron's gone to Italy,' explained Rose from the back.

'Oh, very nice,' remarked Michael.

'She's stowed away.'

'Come again?'

'In her friend's car,' Rose told him. 'Yesterday. We saw them drive past.'

Michael glanced at Caddy to see if this could possibly be true.

Caddy nodded serenely.

'We waved,' Rose went on, 'but of course she couldn't wave back because she was hidden under the bean bag cover.'

'She was?'

'And Mum was very upset when she got home and found out. Very. Very bothered indeed.'

'What about your dad?'

'Haven't told him. Caddy says he need never know.'

'Which way at the roundabout?' asked Caddy peacefully.

'Right. Sorry, I was forgetting. You're in the wrong lane! Indicate! *Don't* barge in front . . . There . . . Missed the road . . . Take no notice of him hooting . . . You can't stop here! Go round again!'

Caddy went round again, and managed to take the right road the next time, frightening Michael, Indigo, Rose and a truck driver in the process.

'I can't believe you just did that,' said Michael.

'That was very, very brave,' agreed Rose, unclamping her fingers from the edge of the seat. 'Zipping in front of that enormous lorry. I'm sorry I screamed.'

'Perfectly natural reaction,' said Michael. 'Have you seen those cyclists ahead, Cadmium?'

'No. Oh yes. Sorry. Shut my eyes for a moment.'

'Can you drive with your eyes shut?' enquired Rose, with great interest.

'No. No, I can't. Missed. Good.'

'Missed what?'

'The cyclists.'

Michael put a hand on the steering wheel and said Caddy should take the next turn on the left and then

107

pull up and park. Caddy pulled into a bus stop and thirteen people waved her away. Rose waved back.

'Count to a hundred,' ordered Michael, when they had escaped from the bus stop and stopped again. 'Get a grip. What's the matter?'

'I think it's having Indigo and Rose in the back. I keep thinking I might kill them.'

'So do we,' said Rose. 'I love it.'

'Good.'

'But Indigo's gone green.'

Caddy and Michael turned hastily round, and saw that this was true. Indigo was definitely green.

'Sick?' asked Michael.

Indigo shook his head.

'Terrified?'

Indigo nodded.

'Worse than the bedroom windowsill?'

Indigo nodded again.

'Wind your window down.'

Indigo wound his window down as far as it would go, and leaned back rather wearily.

'I think we'll go back,' said Michael, and proceeded to talk Caddy home, very slowly and patiently, leaving nothing to chance.

'Aren't we going to do any more speeding?' asked Rose, rather disappointed.

'No,' said Michael.

'Boring,' said Rose, but brightened up a bit when, right outside the Banana House, Caddy pulled up and parked on a large dead toad. The toad went off with a pop, right underneath the open window on Indigo's side. Rose jumped out to inspect the explosion and Indigo jumped out and was sick.

'You were perfectly, perfectly safe,' Caddy told him, mopping his forehead as he lay stretched out on the sofa. 'Michael has a brake on his side, you know. He could have stopped the car any time.'

'I didn't know.'

'And he could always have grabbed the steering wheel. He does, if he has to.'

'Does he?'

'Yes.'

'Does he *often*?'

'No. Hardly ever. And it wasn't my fault about the toad.'

'I know,' said Indigo. 'I know it wasn't your fault about the toad, Caddy.'

'I usually drive *much* better than that.'

'Good,' said Indigo. 'Do you think Saffron's there yet?'

'Nearly, I expect.'

'I keep thinking about her.'

'So do I.'

'Do you think she misses us?'

'No. Not much anyway. She's got Sarah.'

'We don't really know Sarah,' said Indigo, a bit jealously, 'I hope she hasn't pinched Saffy for good!'

'Of course she hasn't,' said Caddy comfortingly. 'She's just borrowed her for a bit.'

★ ★ ★

The day before, Sunday morning, Sarah had passed a note to Saffron. It said,

We are on the road to Siena!!!!!!!!!!!!!!!!!!!!

Sarah had lifted a corner of the bean bag cover so that Saffron should have enough light to read by. The bean bag rustled authentically as it moved. A few handfuls of polystyrene beans had been left inside to give the necessary sound effect. Everything had been thought of.

There had been no hitches. One difficult moment only, when, a day or two before they left, Sarah's mother had come unexpectedly into Sarah's bedroom and noticed the new sports bag.

'Where did you get that?' she had asked.

'Saffron's brother,' said Sarah.

'Rather nice,' said her mother, and the moment had passed.

On the morning of departure, while her parents were rushing round collecting last minute items, Sarah had deliberately got under their feet so often that they had begged her to leave them alone.

'Go and sit in the car, darling. Just until we are ready. We won't be long.'

'How long?'

'Ten minutes.'

During those ten minutes Saffron (concealed in the bushes by the drive) had been smuggled on to the back seat and tucked carefully out of sight under the bean bag. Then a great many bulky items were piled around her, among them Sarah's new padded jacket, two large teddy bears, and a fully assembled box kite.

'You don't show at all!' whispered Sarah proudly.

It was lucky that Sarah's parents were used (as Sarah had remarked to Saffron) to their daughter having a lot of stuff. It hardly surprised them at all.

'Good gracious, Sarah,' her father had commented, as he climbed into the front of the car. 'Will you need all that?'

'It's not as much as it looks,' said Sarah.

'Won't the kite fold flat?' asked her mother.

'No. It's glued.'

'What a silly design!'

'I glued it.'

'That jacket will be far too warm.'

'It's my silver jacket,' said Sarah, sounding slightly mutinous, and then, to prevent any further objections, remarked, 'I wish Saffron was coming!'

'Hmmm,' said her mother, and stopped commenting on the pile of stuff on the back seat.

It was dark and warm under the bean bag, and after the first fifty miles or so, Saffron fell asleep. She was very tired, having not slept much at all the night before. She did not know who she was most frightened of, Sarah's father, who she did not know, or Sarah's mother, who she did. Deciding between them had kept her awake for hours.

Sarah was rather annoyed when she discovered that Saffron was asleep. She had planned a whole series of silent activities for the back seat, including non-rustling snacks, magnetic board games, and notebooks and pencils so that they could write to each other. It seemed a shame that these things might all be wasted.

She prodded Saffron.

Saffron gave a little groan.

She prodded her again.

'Geroff!' said Saffron, quite loudly and distinctly.

'Sarah?' asked her mother.

'What?'

'I thought you said something.'

'Are we nearly there?' asked Sarah, a question deliberately intended to drive her mother to such a state of tension that she forgot everything else. It worked, as it always worked, and Mrs Warbeck got quite hot and bothered explaining that *of course* they were not nearly there, and would not be there for *a day and a half at least*, and that if Sarah was going to ask silly questions every few miles then they might as well turn back *right now*.

'Go to sleep,' suggested her father, and Sarah thought that this might be a sensible thing to do after all. She closed her eyes, and did some pretend snoring, just in case Saffron should make any more noises that needed covering up.

After a while, pretend snoring became too tiring. Sarah was nearly asleep. Just before she was quite, completely asleep she heard her father murmur,

'Pity we didn't bring that little friend!'

Sarah smiled.

★ ★ ★

It was a very long time before Mr Warbeck knew that his wish had come true. He nearly found out on the ferry, when Saffron (provided with an extra car key by Sarah) crept furtively up from the car deck to find a much needed lavatory.

'I've just seen a girl with a nose stud exactly like Sarah's!' Sarah's father had told her mother.

'You see!' said Sarah to her mother. 'I told you everyone had nose studs!'

He might have found out at the French port where they docked. There, Sarah had insisted on handing in the family passports and had added an extra one to the pile, uncovering Saffron for a moment so that she could be inspected by the French official and enter the country legally. This was a very dangerous moment, but it passed successfully. Saffron was covered up again, and miles and miles of France began to pass by, slowly at first, and then faster and faster. It was evening, and they were on the last stretch of motorway before the French hotel where they were to stay the night when Sarah said:

'Guess what!' and unveiled Saffron at last.

'Hullo,' said Saffron nervously.

Sarah's mother said, 'Sarah! Saffron! Saffron! Sarah!'

Sarah said, 'It was totally my idea and I worked it all out and I made her!'

Saffron said, 'I hope you don't mind.'

Sarah's father said, 'Good gracious!'

He did not stop the car; he could not, he had forty kilometres of fast French motorway in front of him before he could do that. He looked behind briefly and drove on.

After a while he said, 'Liz, dear,' reprovingly to Sarah's mother, and she stopped shouting. The car became very silent.

Sarah's father's shoulders began to shake. Tears poured down his cheeks. He took first one hand, and then the other, off the steering wheel to mop his eyes. He drove, weeping and groaning, at a hundred and forty kilometres an hour. Sarah's mother would not look at him. Sarah and Saffron stared, dumbstruck. Then it gradually dawned on them that he was laughing.

After that they knew that everything was going to be all right.

There was still Saffron's family to be told.

'No problem,' said Sarah. 'They know! Well, her sisters and brother know. And I told Saffy to leave a note for her mother . . .'

'Did you do that, Saffron?' demanded Mrs Warbeck.

'It was so hard to think of anything to say,' said Saffron. 'Without being worrying. So in the end . . . in the end . . .'

'Yes?'

'I just came away.'

'Saffron!'

'She won't mind at all!' said Saffron.

This was not true. Eve was, as Rose had informed Michael the next day, very upset. And very bothered.

Very bothered indeed. Caddy and Indigo and Rose found it quite difficult to get her safely into her shed that night.

'Paint!' cooed Caddy. 'Painting always makes you feel better! I will look after Indigo and Rose.'

'I will make you a cup of tea with gin in it,' promised Indigo.

'I will get rid of Daddy if he rings and asks to speak to Saffy,' said Rose.

Eve allowed herself to be led to her shed, drank her cup of tea, blew her nose on a paint rag, and said she didn't know what Rose could possibly say to Daddy that would get rid of him.

'I will ask him about Art,' said Rose placidly.

'Darling Rose!' said Eve gratefully. 'Oh, I wish I understood Saffron! I don't know why she had to go away like that. I have gone terribly wrong with Saffron!'

'She had to go,' said Rose.

'It was because of her angel,' said Indigo.

'And because of Grandad,' added Caddy.

'And because of her nose stud.'

'And because her name isn't on the colour chart.'

'She's lonely,' said Rose. 'That's why.'

Chapter Nine

It was a long, long way from England to Siena. Sarah's father did the driving, despite many pleas from Sarah's mother to be allowed to take a turn while he had a rest.

'Wouldn't be a rest at all!' he said. 'Far from it! You sit back and look out of the window. I'm enjoying myself! I only came for the drive!'

They travelled right across France and into the Alps. Then through a terrible tunnel.

'I remember this tunnel,' exclaimed Saffron, startling everyone in the car, because all across France and into the mountains she had hardly said a word.

'I've been this way before,' she added, and she thought what an endless journey it must have been for her grandfather with his daughter dead, and a three year old who would not stop crying, and a car full of toys.

'You've been to Italy?' asked Mrs Warbeck, astonished, and Sarah said,

'Saffy was born in Siena,' and went on to tell the story of how Saffron had lost her mother and come to the Banana House, ten years before.

'Have you the address of where you used to live?'

asked Sarah's mother, sounding quite excited. 'Do you know where it was? You must want to find it again!'

'She's got the address written down,' said Sarah, jumping in before Saffron could speak for herself. 'I told her to bring it.'

'I should keep well clear if I were you, Saffy!' said Sarah's father. 'Never go back! It'll not be the way you remember it.'

'I don't suppose Saffy does remember it,' said Mrs Warbeck.

'I remember the garden,' said Saffy, a bit shyly, and she gave Sarah a look that meant, Don't mention the stone angel!

Sarah did not need the warning. She had a feeling that securing Saffy's angel might not be very easy. She was almost prepared to steal it, if necessary, but she thought that this was something her parents would be happier not to know.

'If you had explained to us about Saffron being born in Siena we should have loved to invite her to come with us!' Sarah's mother told Sarah a little crossly. 'Since we had decided to come anyway, it would have been the obvious thing to do! Why ever did you have to make everything so difficult?'

'You were so mad about my nose stud,' said Sarah.

'Mad about your nose stud?' repeated Mrs Warbeck, and she began to laugh and laugh. She laughed like Sarah's father had done when Sarah had pulled back the bean bag cover and said, 'Guess what?' Sarah's father joined in.

Saffron and Sarah looked at them, and then they looked at each other. They were totally mystified.

They reached their hotel in Siena late on Monday night.

By this time, back at the Banana House, people were feeling better again. Eve was fast asleep in her shed, curled up on the old pink sofa. She had finished another painting (*Sunlight On The Water*). In it a tropical sun beamed down on the town park duck pond (miraculously Coca-Cola can free, for once) and a girl who looked very like Saffron (but with no nose stud) smiled contentedly down at the water lilies and showed no sign of running away.

Rose was still awake, late though it was. She was painting a vast desert landscape on the white landing wall. She had got rid of her father very successfully when he telephoned. Saffron had hardly been mentioned, the discussion had been all about Art. The desert landscape was the direct result of her father telling her to start small and stick to painting only what she knew.

Indigo was more or less recovered from his reaction to Caddy's driving and he also was still awake. He was testing Caddy on the Highway Code. At teatime Michael had telephoned to tell them there was a cancellation at the Driving Test centre, and Caddy could take her exam on Friday afternoon.

'You have had ninety-six lessons,' said Michael. 'I counted up. It has cost your dad one thousand, four hundred and twenty-five pounds because the first one was free.'

'Michael, darling!' said Caddy, shocked. 'Have you actually charged my poor father one thousand, four hundred and twenty-five pounds?'

'Yep! And don't call me darling, I'm a driving instructor.'

'And has he paid you?'

'Of course. I send a bill once a month. But this afternoon when I got in there was a letter from him saying enough was enough. And he is right. That's why I wangled the Test Centre to let you in on Friday.'

Caddy moaned.

'And it works out very well because I am away on holiday next week so I couldn't take you out anyway. I am off to Spain . . .'

'With Droopy Di?'

'So when you have passed (which you naturally will because I am a fantastic teacher and Diane passed after only ten lessons), I shall leave the car with you for the week. Since I won't be needing it and you are my favourite pupil . . .'

'Pupil!'

'You can drive yourself off to your college exams. Get in a bit of practice. You will be fine if you don't panic. So I will see you on Friday afternoon.'

'Michael, you can't possibly think I will pass my driving test on Friday afternoon!'

'Why ever not?'

'I just don't pass exams. I never have.'

'Well, you had better start now!' said Michael robustly. 'It is either begin passing exams, or a future as a small scale guinea pig farmer living at home with no transport. So think about that, Cadmium darling!'

There was a long pause.

'Cadmium, *what*?' asked Caddy at last.

'Well. All right. Darling. Since you insist, darling.'

'Cadmium darling!' said Caddy, whirling round the kitchen. 'Cadmium darling! Indigo!'

'Yes?'

'Can you see me as a small scale guinea pig farmer living at home with no transport?'

'No,' said Indigo at once.

'Perhaps,' said Caddy hopefully, 'you don't have to drive very well to pass your driving test. Perhaps you just have to be OK. OKish.'

'That must be it,' agreed Indigo.

Saffron awoke in a room striped with sunlight. Early morning Italian sunshine was pouring through the gaps in the closed shutters at the window, and making bands of brightness on the walls. In a bed on the opposite side of the room, Sarah was also awake. Saffron saw that there was a look of intense concentration on her friend's face, and that she was behaving very oddly, struggling on her back as if fighting to throw off some enormous invisible weight. When she saw Saffron looking at her she closed her eyes and went limp against the pillows.

'Are you all right?' asked Saffron.

'I've got stuck,' said Sarah, not opening her eyes.

'What?'

Sarah said resignedly, 'My back's so stiff and my legs have gone stupid. I can't sit up.'

The long car journey had left Saffron stiff too, but not so stiff that she could not move. She slid out of bed and went across to help.

'If I can roll over and get my elbow under me I can do it,' explained Sarah. 'I'm OK when I get started.'

'I'll push.'

'Good old Super Hero.'

It was quite hard work. It left them both breathless for a minute.

'It's gravity,' explained Sarah, when she was propped up against her pillows. 'It picks on me! It holds me down more than it does other people! I must have natural magnetism.'

Saffron thought for a moment and then said, 'You need vertical take off pyjamas.'

'You are absolutely right,' agreed Sarah instantly. 'What time is it?'

'Half past seven.'

'Open the shutters and let's look out. We made it! Siena! I told you we would!'

Saffron crossed the room, opened the window and pushed back the shutters, and watched affectionately as Sarah tottered across the floor to join her.

'I'm drunk,' she said, waving her arms to balance herself.

'Try not to fall out of the window, Mission Control,' said Saffron.

'Excellent advice, Super Hero,' said Sarah, collapsing beside her.

The hotel was on one side of a large square of buildings, little shops, and cafés with umbrellas and outside tables. There were red tiled roofs in every direction and beyond the red tiles there were green and blue hills under a blue Italian sky.

Sarah and Saffron immediately appropriated it all.

'Gosh, look! We've got a fountain!'

'And a painted church,' said Saffron, looking across the square.

'What are the pictures?'

'Angels,' said Saffron, who always noticed angels.

'They must have known we were coming.'

'We've got a lot of flowers.'

'And about ten thousand pigeons.'

'They must have worked hard.'

'Catching them all.'

'Mmmm. In the night.'

There was a pause.

'Well?' asked Sarah, expectantly.

'What?'

'Do you remember it?'

'No,' said Saffron.

'No?'

'They must have changed it.'

'Saffron,' said Sarah. 'Everything outside this window except the pigeons looks at least six centuries old.'

'I've been away a long time,' said Saffron mournfully.

Sarah's mother came in while they were still recovering from this remark.

'I knocked,' she said, 'but I just heard shrieking! Did you sleep well? Are you all right Sarah? I was afraid you'd be terribly stiff.'

'I'm fine,' said Sarah, as cheerfully as if she had never had an ache in her life. 'Not a bit stiff. Look at the lovely fountain! Squirting dragons!'

'Lions,' said her mother, after a careful look.

'They've got wings,' said Sarah.

'Those are their manes!' said Mrs Warbeck, and then both she and Sarah turned to Saffron and asked, Lions or Dragons, as if she was the Siena expert.

'Lions,' decided Saffron, and Sarah said, 'OK, lions. You're the one who was born here. You ought to know.'

'I don't really remember anything,' said Saffron, but as the morning went on she found that this was not quite true.

'I remember the voices,' she said, out in the market square inspecting the lions with Sarah and her mother, while Italian voices were calling and talking all around them. 'I can't understand them, but I remember they sounded like that. And I remember the sunshine.'

'It is like best quality English sunshine,' agreed Sarah's mother.

'But, Super Hero,' said Sarah sternly. 'Don't you remember where you lived?'

'Of course she doesn't!' said Mrs Warbeck, laughing. 'She was three! But we'll find it, Saffron. Don't worry. Perhaps we could get a taxi and go there today.'

'Hmmm,' said Sarah.

'Hmmm, what?' asked her mother suspiciously.

'Only I thought Saffron and I could go by ourselves,' said Sarah. 'You don't have to come with us, Mummy dear. We could manage a taxi perfectly well. Everyone here understands English if you shout loud enough . . .'

'Sarah!'

'I'm only saying what Dad said last night!'

Mrs Warbeck said she was sure that Sarah's father had said no such thing, and that if she heard Sarah shouting English at *anyone*, she would lock her in her room till Friday. Also that under no circumstances would she and Saffron be let loose to explore Siena alone by taxi. She said these things quite cheerfully, however, much less sternly than she would have done at home.

'She doesn't have to act like the Private School Head here,' Sarah told Saffron, explaining her mother's holiday behaviour. 'She's just a plain tourist, like everybody else! She changes on holiday. Not like Dad. He stays exactly the same. He finds somewhere to put his lap-top and he buys an English newspaper, and at every meal he passes my mother the menu and says to choose him something plain!'

'Why does he come then?'

'He likes driving very fast on the wrong side of the

road,' said Sarah. 'Which I can completely understand.'

At lunchtime Sarah was proved to be correct. Her mother produced a sheaf of coloured leaflets of all they might do and said, 'Let's choose what we absolutely cannot bear to miss.'

'OK,' said Sarah's father. 'But spare me Art. And History. Is there anything simple on that menu?'

(Sarah smirked and caught Saffron's eye.)

'Lots of lovely things. Pasta?'

'Rubber,' said Sarah's father. 'Dressed up rubber, that's what pasta is. Everyone thinks so, but no one dares say it except me.'

Sarah's mother had heard this opinion several dozen times before so she ignored it and said,

'All right. No art. No history. No pasta. Shopping?'

'Gosh no!' said Mr Warbeck, sounding terribly shocked. 'Shopping! No thank you. I can order everything I want from the Internet.'

'What about going into the countryside?'

'Don't mind a picnic,' said Mr Warbeck. 'So long as I don't have to pretend to admire the view. What are you girls giggling about? Is that supposed to be a plain salad, Liz? You've let them put dressing all over it.'

'You eat salad dressing at home,' said Sarah's mother, and Sarah's father said yes, but now he was on holiday and could do what he liked, and they should go off and leave him to it.

'Are you just going to stay in the hotel the whole afternoon?' asked his wife.

'I may take a stroll out to have a look at those

squirting dragons across there,' said Mr Warbeck. 'That fountain is very badly set up. It is losing water all the time. I've noticed already. It's the angle of that top jet. You get off and enjoy yourselves and don't worry about me. They're setting me up with a phone line and a table that doesn't wobble this afternoon. Very helpful, I must say. Look them in the eye and shout and they understand every word . . .'

Sarah and Saffron collapsed with laughter.

'I brought you a phrase book,' said his wife crossly, jumping up. 'It's in our room. I should have tied it round your neck! I'll go and fetch it now!'

'She should have been a diplomat,' said Mr Warbeck, looking affectionately after her. 'What do you two want to do this afternoon then? Art? Shopping? History? Admire the landscape? Spot of bull fighting? No, that's Spain, I think.'

'We're going to find Saffy's home, of course,' Sarah told him, adding thoughtlessly, 'that was the whole idea of coming to Siena in the first place!'

'Was it?' asked Mr Warbeck, mildly, while Saffron blushed redder and redder. 'Was it indeed? I did wonder.'

'Don't tell Mum!' begged Sarah. 'She thinks she thought of coming here! I didn't mean to say that!'

'I refuse to be involved in your conspiracies,' said Mr Warbeck. 'And you know what I told you, never go back. Still, if you must, you must, I suppose. Good luck, Saffy!'

'Thank you,' said Saffy.

That afternoon Mrs Warbeck put Sarah, Saffron and the wheelchair in the back of a taxi, got in the front herself, gave the taxi driver Saffron's old address in Siena and asked for them to be taken there.

The taxi driver looked at her as if she was mad.

She repeated it more slowly, carefully not shouting. He still looked bemused.

She handed him the piece of paper on which it was written down and asked if he understood it.

'*Si, si*,' he said nodding.

'*Grazie!*' said Mrs Warbeck, very firmly, and she leaned back against her seat to indicate that she would like to be obeyed, and without any further fuss.

The taxi driver shrugged his shoulders and steered out of the square, down a side road and round a corner. Then he stopped. They had been driving quite slowly for about one minute.

'Is there a problem?' asked Mrs Warbeck, politely but quite loudly.

The taxi driver said, no, no, there was no problem, they had arrived.

This took quite a while to sink in, and it was not until the taxi driver had climbed out of the taxi and pointed very forcefully to the sign at the corner *Via S. Francesco* that Mrs Warbeck would get out of her seat, and pay the bill, and turn and look where Sarah and Saffron were already staring.

'It's Number Sixteen,' said Saffron.

There in the street, outside a faded green door in a

brown plastered wall, Saffron began to cry. She did not know why she was crying. Perhaps she was tired. Perhaps she had thought of her angel too much and for too long. Perhaps it was because this was where she had lived with her mother, and one day had walked away from, and had never come back.

Sarah and her mother waited patiently, while the tears poured down Saffron's cheeks. They did not seem at all surprised, and they did not tell her to stop crying. Sarah sat in her wheelchair doing nothing at all, while her mother silently handed over paper hanky after paper hanky from a seemingly endless supply in her bag.

After a while Sarah moved away to look at the house more closely, searching for the way that would lead round to the garden. It was the corner house of a block of little houses, rather shabby, but with bright flowery window boxes at its upstairs windows. It was built directly on to the street. That meant the windows in two of the walls could be seen. They were painted green like the door and their shutters were closed. It was impossible to walk round the back of the house because it was joined straight on to the one next to it.

Unseen by her mother, Sarah wheeled herself back round the corner into the street they had driven down. At first there seemed to be no way around to any garden on that side either; the wall ran on solidly all down the length of the block. Then Sarah noticed a door in the wall, painted the same faded green as the front door and the shutters. She hurried back to Saffron and waited for a pause between handkerchiefs.

'I've found the garden door!' she said, when one came at last. 'But I'm afraid it's locked . . .'

'Sarah! You didn't try to open it!' interrupted her mother.

'Of course I tried to open it. First thing!' said Sarah. 'I wanted to see Saffy's angel . . .' She stopped suddenly, remembering that her mother knew nothing about any angels, but Mrs Warbeck had not noticed.

'You were very rude! You should at least have knocked!' she told her severely.

'All right,' said Sarah cheerfully. 'I'll go back and knock.'

'I'm coming too,' said Saffron, accepting a last paper handkerchief. 'Wait for me. I'm sorry I cried.'

Sarah waited, saying encouragingly, while Saffron mopped her nose, 'I read once that you can only cry thirty-eight tears at a time. Thirty-eight maximum. Then they stop.'

'Good.'

'That's what I thought,' agreed Sarah. 'Of course, it's practically impossible to count . . . You need a cold-blooded observer to tell you how long you've got to go . . . Look! I bet anything that's the garden door!'

'It must be,' agreed Saffron at once.

It was a heavy old door with a metal latch, set under an arch of wall. It was, as Sarah had already discovered, firmly locked. Nobody came when they knocked. Nobody answered at the front door either. Nor at the next house along in the street. Nobody looked out of a window, or walked past and asked what they were doing, knocking and knocking on all those doors.

In desperation Saffron and Sarah got down on their hands and knees and tried to see under the crack at the bottom of the garden door.

'Whatever would you say if someone saw you?' scolded Sarah's mother when she saw what they were doing.

'We would say "This is the house where Saffron used to live and she wanted to see in the garden."'

'We will call again,' promised Mrs Warbeck. 'I'm sure we will find someone in another day. Come on now, let's go back to the square and find Daddy. I hope he hasn't been shouting at too many people!'

Mr Warbeck was not shouting at anybody, he was peacefully reading a newspaper on a seat by the fountain, looking completely at home. He waved when he saw them, took one look at Saffron's face, and led the way to one of the little café tables under the umbrellas. There he ordered ice creams and taught them to play a disgraceful game, which consisted of awarding marks out of ten for Italian bottoms.

'First one to spot a genuine ten chooses the next round of ice cream,' he said to Saffy and Sarah. 'Liz can referee.'

'I'll do no such thing!' said Mrs Warbeck.

'There might not be a ten in the whole of Italy!' objected Sarah.

'A ten or a nine then,' said her father. 'Be warned though, the ref must agree.'

'I think eights should count too,' said Sarah.

'Oh, all right. Fair enough.'

'Sevens?' asked Sarah.

'Not a hope,' said her father firmly. 'Eights are the absolute minimum!'

He and Sarah glared at each other, looking so alike that Saffron could not help laughing.

'Concentrate!' Sarah's father told her sternly. 'There! Look there! I've seen a nine already! OK ref?'

'No,' said Mrs Warbeck. 'That was not a nine. Far from a nine. Six perhaps . . .'

It was a very good game, and went on for nearly two hours, and although nobody spotted a ten there were several eights and nines to argue about. Later they went out for a drive and had supper in a place where Sarah's father said the only thing edible was the bread, and by the time they got back Saffron's mind was a muddle of hills and olive trees and food and fountains and Italian bottoms.

'Sweet dreams, Saffy!' said Mr Warbeck, when the girls went up to bed that night.

Saffron dreamt of the garden behind the green door. And her grandfather's hand in hers. And the angel in the garden, the stone angel from Siena, a long time ago. It was exactly the same dream as always. Nothing had changed.

Chapter Ten

Sarah's mother had promised that Saffron would ring home every day. This happened, starting the first Sunday evening when Sarah revealed the stowaway in the back of the family car.

That first time Saffron had spoken only to Eve, explaining that she was not, as Eve had supposed until she answered the phone, upstairs in her bedroom, but on the contrary was six hundred miles from home, in a faraway French hotel.

By that time the Banana House already felt to Saffron like somewhere she had known briefly and long ago, in a different life, in a different world. Then Eve answered the telephone and Saffron heard her familiar 'Saffy darling,' and it occurred to Saffron for the first time that Eve might mind her going without a word of goodbye or explanation. She might be upset. She might be hurt.

'Hello,' said Saffron, uncertainly. It was very bad to think that Eve might be hurt. Angry and worried were nothing in comparison.

'Saffy darling!' said Eve again. 'Saffy darling! Saffy darling, *where are you?*'

'Sarah's father says about halfway,' said Saffron. 'Didn't Caddy tell you?'

'Sarah's father? Caddy?'

'Where is Caddy?' asked Saffron desperately. 'She could tell you much better than me!'

'Caddy and Indigo and Rose are all out. The guinea pigs escaped this afternoon. All over the road. So they're all three out rounding up . . . *Halfway to where?*'

'Siena.'

'Siena?'

'Siena in Italy.'

'Siena in Italy?'

'But you needn't worry . . .'

'Needn't worry!'

Then the conversation had reversed backwards. *Needn't worry! Siena in Italy! Siena! Saffy darling!*

'Sarah's mother would like a quick word!' interrupted Saffron, and she pushed the telephone into Mrs Warbeck's hand, with such an anguished face that Sarah's mother said, 'All right, Saffron,' and proceeded to explain, as best she could, how Saffron had come to be where she was, and how they would bring her straight back if necessary, but would love to have her otherwise, and how they would all laugh about this One Day. And that Eve was not to worry. Not to worry, not to worry, not to worry.

That was the Sunday telephone call. It went on for a long time. The Monday one, however, was answered by Rose, and was very brief indeed.

'She says she's got there,' reported Rose, relaying the

conversation across the kitchen, 'but it's too dark to see anything! Oh well. 'Night, Saffy!'

'Rose!' exclaimed everyone, but they were too late. Rose had already put down the phone.

'Rose!' wailed Eve.

'Mmmm?' said Rose, absentmindedly licking some paint she had just noticed on the palm of her hand.

'You shouldn't have cut her off like that! I would have liked to talk to her! I wanted to tell her I wasn't cross!'

'She'll know that,' said Rose, licking her hand once more and then rubbing it on her jeans.

'I wanted to ask what it was like, to be back in Siena,' said Caddy.

'Dark,' Rose reminded her. 'I told you.'

'Even so,' said Eve, 'You did pounce on the phone very quickly, Rose darling!'

'I had to pounce,' said Rose, 'in case it was Daddy. You might have told him about Saffy by accident.'

'I suppose I might,' agreed Eve.

On Tuesday evening, luckily when Eve was safely out and Rose was alone in the kitchen, her father called to say that he had just realised it was half term, and since he had a gap in his schedule he might come home and spend some time with his family. Or pop over to France for some duty free. Whichever.

'Pop over to France,' said Rose instantly, having grabbed the telephone at the very first ring.

'Oh?' said her father, a little taken aback to be under attack so soon in the conversation.

'Well, it's no good coming home. Everyone's so busy.'

'Busy?' said Bill, laughingly, saying without words that Rose should know quite well he was the only one who ever did any work in the family.

'Caddy just revises for exams,' said Rose. 'All those exams you made her do. Remember?'

'Oh yes. Well, yes.'

'And Indigo's doing a lot of cooking.'

'Yes?'

'A lot of cooking. To keep Caddy's strength up, he says.'

'Right.'

'And I'm painting my desert mural.'

'Oh are you?'

'And Saffron . . .' Rose paused. Saffron was quite difficult.

'Yes?' said her father, sensing a whiff of conquest. 'Yes? Saffron?'

'She's out all day. With her friend. All day. We haven't really seen her at all.'

'Since when?'

'Saturday,' said Rose, triumphantly truthful.

'Mummy won't be busy,' said Rose's father, and Rose sighed with relief because Eve was easy.

'She is the busiest of everyone. Because of her exhibition.'

'What exhibition?' demanded Bill, astonished and a little put out, because he was the one who did exhibitions, not Eve.

'In the Building Society window.'

'Oh, that!'

'People keep buying the pictures so she has to keep doing more and more. It's a problem, she says.'

It was not a problem that Bill often had with his exhibitions, so he did not say anything.

'Because the window keeps looking empty and the manager complains.'

'She shouldn't let the people take them away,' said Bill a bit peevishly. 'She is obviously not charging enough. Fetch her. I want to talk to her.'

'I can't fetch her,' said Rose. She spoke quite gently now, because this was victory. 'She's gone to the bank. She has to keep going to the bank to put the picture money in. Then when she comes back she has to paint more pictures. So.'

'I see,' said Bill, hurt, annoyed and deflated. 'Well then, I will get back to work.'

'I thought you were popping over to France.'

'That was just a thought,' said Bill, with dignity. 'I have a great deal of on-going work.'

'Bye, then Daddy,' said Rose sweetly, waving into the receiver.

'Bye, Rose,' said Bill.

That was Bill sorted out for the week, and they could concentrate on Saffron.

That same Tuesday night she had telephoned to say they had found the house in Siena where she used to live.

'Oh, Saffy,' said Eve. 'Are you all right?'

'Quite all right,' said Saffron. 'Don't worry!'

★   ★   ★

On Wednesday she told them about the cathedral that Sarah's mother had insisted they visit. Also about the way she and Sarah were allowed to explore the square and the little shops around it by themselves, and how already the ice cream man knew their names and remembered which flavours they had tried and said, 'No! No!' and made them choose another if they selected the same one twice.

'She sounds like she's having a lovely time,' said Caddy wistfully.

Caddy was not having a lovely time herself. Indigo had pointed out that since she had stopped going into college no physics revision was taking place at all. To counteract this he had helped her stick physics notes on to every window of the Banana House.

The windows had been Caddy's last refuge. Now each of them held a different branch of physics and there was no direction in which she could look without learning something.

Nor had there been any comfort from Michael. He had turned up unexpectedly on Wednesday morning and taken her out on a surprise mock driving test, which Caddy thought had probably been even more stressful than the real thing itself would be.

At least, she told Indigo and Rose, when she staggered back in again, the examiner taking her on the real test would not be unkindly comparing her with his gorgeous, heroic, talented and hard-working girlfriend at every roundabout and junction. Which had been all Michael would talk about (apart from gear changes).

'But did he say you would have passed?' demanded Indigo.

'Oh yes.'

'Well then. That's brilliant.'

'She's sad because he didn't say "Caddy darling",' Rose explained patiently to him. 'He's got this weird old girlfriend called Droopy Di so he can't have our Caddy.'

'He can't have our Caddy anyway!' said Indigo, indignantly.

He can if he wants, thought Caddy, as she bent over the black and white diagrams of the structure of the mammalian heart in her biology book. Biologists, thought Caddy, rapidly sketching in the paths of blood circulation with red and blue pencils, make it seem so simple. The same heart whoever you are, hamster or human, and no reference in the whole book to the Effects and Consequences of falling in love.

'Did you think Saffron sounded happy when you talked to her?' Indigo asked, interrupting the red and blue pencils, and Caddy, after a moment of surprised thought, said, 'No.'

'She would have done, if she'd found her angel,' said Indigo.

'Yes,' agreed Rose. 'And if she hasn't found her angel she won't care a bit about cathedrals and ice cream and all that stuff.'

'She'd just be saying that for something to say,' agreed Indigo.

'It's hard to tell how anyone really feels from a telephone call,' pointed out Caddy. 'People use happy voices when they're sad, and tired voices when they're thinking . . . We'll just have to wait. Perhaps everything is perfectly all right.'

'I bet it isn't,' said Rose.

Rose, as usual, was right. What had mattered most to Saffron, that Wednesday in Siena, had been the closed green doors and windows of the house where once she had lived. She and Sarah had not just explored the square together. Over and over again they had made their way back to Number Sixteen, Via S. Francesco. They had pressed their faces against the cracks in the locked garden door. Saffron, remembering the noise of running water that went with her dream, had stood motionless, straining to hear the sound again. They had seen and heard nothing. That was what had been wrong with that Wednesday for Saffron. And also the fact that everywhere she went she saw other people's angels.

Sarah noticed them too and said, 'No wonder you were so fond of yours! They seem to have been in fashion here for about eight hundred years!'

On Thursday when Saffron rang home, she told them in detail the story of Sarah's father and his triumph with the fountain. Saffron explained how Mr Warbeck had been talking with the hotel manager (in good loud English with plenty of eye contact). And how Mr

Warbeck had remarked that although the hotel was excellent and everything was fine, the fountain in the centre of the square was causing him considerable distress. The angle of the top jet, said Mr Warbeck, was out by possibly as much as five degrees (here he produced a piece of paper with a sketch he had made), and the water lost, he had calculated (and here was the calculation), must be several gallons a day. Or litres, of course. A lot anyway. And the adjustment needed was so simple (Mr Warbeck produced a third piece of paper illustrating the necessary correction) that it really ought to be dealt with before he, Mr Warbeck, was driven mad. In England, explained Sarah's father, you would call the town council and have it put right because you paid your taxes to have things run properly.

Astonishingly, (at least, it astonished Sarah's father) it seemed that in Italy things were much the same. Because the hotel manager took away Mr Warbeck's pieces of paper and made a telephone call, and later that day an engineer came out. And with a wrench and a ladder and Mr Warbeck's diagrams he made the alteration required. And now the people in the hotel were treating Sarah's father as a hero, and the Warbecks had had free wine sent to their table, and Sarah's father said the age of miracles was not yet over and the Italians were fine and efficient people. You might wait weeks before it was fixed in England, he said, and there would be no free wine attached either.

This was what Saffron told Caddy and Indigo and Rose on Thursday. No mention of her old home. No mention of angels. This time there was no need for Indigo to ask, 'Do you think Saffron sounded happy?' because there was no doubt about it. She sounded miserable.

'We're coming home tomorrow,' she had told Caddy. 'Tomorrow afternoon.'

'Saffron,' said Caddy. 'Have you been back to the house? Your house, I mean.'

'Of course I have.'

'Well, have you seen into the garden? Have you *been* in the garden? Have you *tried*? What about your . . .'

'The door is locked!' snapped Saffron. 'Of course I've been! Of course I've tried! The door is always locked and we're leaving tomorrow!'

'Don't cry, Saffy!'

'I'm not,' said Saffron, and slammed down the phone.

Mr and Mrs Warbeck noticed how subdued Saffron was that evening, but kindly put it down to a combination of tiredness, the emotion of seeing her old home again, and worry because the holiday was nearly over and soon she would be back at the Banana House, explaining why she had stowed away in someone else's car without even leaving a note to say goodbye.

Sarah understood. She knew the truth was that the green shuttered house on the corner behind the square was filling Saffron's thoughts. She and Saffron had been back to it very often now. Every odd

141

moment, before outings, after meals, between shops and ice creams and photographs by the fountain (leaking and unleaking) they had made dashes to the house. Sometimes Saffron had gone alone, but more often Sarah had been with her, bumping across the cobbles and along the narrow pavement in her wheelchair, faster every time. They had knocked, but no one answered. The shutters were always closed and the doors were always locked.

Sarah lay in bed very late on Thursday night and thought about the house. She thought and thought and finally she called softly across the bedroom,

'Super Hero! Wake up!'

'I am awake,' replied Saffron at once. 'I thought you were asleep.'

'I've got a plan.'

'Oh.'

'Somebody lives there.'

Saffron did not ask where Sarah was talking about because she knew perfectly well.

'Somebody lives there,' continued Sarah. 'Think of the flowers in the window boxes upstairs. Somebody waters those flowers.'

Saffron hoisted herself up on one elbow and looked across at Sarah. She was right, somebody must water the flowers.

'Perhaps they are on holiday,' she suggested.

'No,' said Sarah. 'I bet those flowers are watered every day. Same as the ones in the square. Early in the morning, I've heard them doing it. And that's when we ought to go. Before whoever waters the flowers goes out.'

'We could try.'

'I must see into that garden before we go home!' said Sarah, forgetting to whisper in her earnestness. 'I must see if your angel is there. If it is, there's all sorts of things we could do. There might be a way of buying it. We could ask my parents to help. Anything would be better than coming away and not ever knowing if it was still there.'

'I think so too,' said Saffron. 'I've been trying to work out how I could climb the wall. Even if I could only get high enough to look over the top for a moment it would be something. If I began at the house, with your chair to start me off, and then stepped on to the windowsill, perhaps I could use the shutters somehow to get me high enough to get a hold on the top of the wall. Then I would have to swing across somehow. If I could get my arms over I think I could do it . . .'

Saffron paused. Sarah's eyes were quite startling. Huge and shining and fixed on Saffron's face as she visualised this epic ascent. In the shadows of her dark hair, her face was as white as her pillows, the hot Italian sunshine had not touched it at all. She looked very small. A small pattern of shadows in a big bed. Sarah could not climb the wall by way of windowsill and shutters, but she did not say so. She had hoped herself for an early morning miracle, somebody watering flowers.

'What could I do?' she asked. 'While you were climbing.'

'You would have to wait,' said Saffron, and as soon as she had said the words she wished she could unsay them. After all, climbing the wall would be the very last bit of the long adventure, planned by Sarah, that had brought them to Siena. And Sarah would be left out of it. Suddenly Saffron had a picture in her mind of Sarah waiting at the bottom of the wall, and she was angry with herself.

Something in Saffron changed at that moment. She knew all about feeling left out. Ever since the afternoon when she was eight and had read the paint chart in the Banana House kitchen she had known that feeling. It had been even worse when her grandfather died and it seemed that she had been left out again. That was why she had wanted her angel so badly; proof that she mattered as much as anyone else.

'I couldn't really climb that wall,' she said. 'And if I could, what if I got caught? What would I say?'

'You'd think of something.'

'No. It was a stupid idea. Let's try your way, early in the morning.'

'Before breakfast?'

'Yes. All right, Mission Control?'

'All right,' said Sarah. 'All right, Super Hero.'

At the Banana House only Indigo and Rose were asleep. Eve had gone to bed, but her mind was on something she had bought for herself that morning. It

144

was her reward for her success in the Building Society window, a large new canvas, a handful of new brushes, and four new enormous tubes of oils.

After a while Eve could resist the temptation no longer. She sneaked down the stairs and out to the shed. It was one o'clock in the morning. Friday. On Friday Saffron would begin the long journey home. Eve thought of them lovingly, one by one. Cadmium, Saffron, Indigo, Rose. Soon they would all be together again.

Caddy could not sleep because Friday was the day of her driving test. This was very scary in itself, but made worse by the fact that if she passed she would probably never see Michael again because she wouldn't be having any more lessons. If she failed she would definitely never see him again. For one thing, Michael wouldn't want to have anything to do with her: he liked glittering successes like Droopy Di who passed first time. And for another thing, her father had said several times recently that if Caddy could not pass after nearly a hundred lessons with an instructor there must be something badly wrong with him, and they would have to try someone else instead. Someone older.

'Michael is old,' Rose had told her father when she happened to hear this opinion. 'He is twenty-four.'

'*Much* older,' said Rose's father. 'My age.'

'Oh,' said Rose. '*That* old. *Very* old. Poor Caddy!'

Chapter Eleven

The little square looked different in the early morning sunlight.

'It's the shadows,' said Saffron. 'They're in different places. And there are less people.'

'No tourists,' said Sarah.

'Except us.'

'We're not tourists,' said Sarah. 'You're not anyway, you were born here! And look how people are beginning to get to know us!'

It was true, in a way. Smiles and waves of recognition from the shop and café owners getting ready for the new day followed them around the square. Sarah and Saffron smiled and waved back at them until the sight of somebody with a hose pipe watering tubs of geraniums gave them a sudden sense of urgency.

'Come on!' said Sarah, and they hurried away from the sunny square, on down the familiar side street, deserted as usual, and turned the corner.

'There!' said Sarah, a moment later, and she pointed in triumph.

The flowers in the window boxes were sparkling

and wet. Splashes were falling past the open green shutters and landing all around. Clearly they had been watered only a minute or two before.

'Let's knock,' suggested Sarah.

'Let's try the garden door first,' said Saffron.

They left the dripping flowers and went back round the corner to the garden door and Saffron reached up to the big iron ring that lifted the latch. They had tried it so often since Sarah's first attempt that it no longer seemed a wrong thing to do.

'It's turning!' Saffron said, almost whispering. 'It's open! Are we going in?'

'Of course,' said Sarah, impatiently. 'What do you think we came here for?'

Saffron pushed the door wide open.

It was a little white paved garden. Small pointed trees in tubs. The sound of water falling from a miniature fountain, a bright blue sky above and walls all around. They heard a voice call out sharply, and then hurrying footsteps. A tiny old woman, dark haired and wrinkled, appeared from the back of the house and came running towards them, calling all the time in very fast Italian.

Suddenly, she paused as if frozen, and then began running and calling again, but this time her words were English, 'Stay! Stay! Wait!'

Sarah guessed what was happening straight away, but Saffron, caught in a tangle of past and present, was too confused to do anything but stand and stare.

'Wait! After so long! After so long, Linda's Saffron!'

exclaimed the old lady, and Sarah, who knew that Linda was Saffron's mother's name, realised that her friend had been recognised almost at once.

'Linda's Saffron!' repeated the old lady, suddenly sweeping Saffron into her arms for a hug, and then standing back again to look at her. 'Saffron!' and she began laughing and crying and patting Saffron's cheeks.

'Linda was my mother,' said Saffron, speaking at last.

'*Si, si*, and you are Saffron and you are so exactly like her that I knew you at once! Like Linda! But you were so young when you went away, I think you have forgotten Antonia who lived above you?'

'I think I've forgotten everything,' said Saffron, and she looked and sounded dazed as she spoke. 'Everything except the garden.'

'You remember the garden?'

'Yes,' said Saffron, as she gazed around. 'I thought it was bigger, but I do remember it. Is it your garden?'

'*Si, si*. My house and garden. I live upstairs and you and your mamma live downstairs. You play in the garden, all day long.'

'Do you mind me coming back? We just came in. We should have knocked.'

The old lady who was Antonia swept Saffron back into her arms again and said of course she did not mind, of course not, of course not! Nor for the friend. Was it not Saffron's home, and why had she not come back years before, and where did she live now? And how was her grandfather? And would anyone believe how often and often Antonia had come into the garden and thought of Saffron and her angel?

'My *angel*?' repeated Saffron.

Antonia said, '*Si, si*, her angel in the garden.'

'Saffy's angel?' asked Sarah eagerly. 'What about Saffy's angel?'

'Her little stone angel,' said Antonia, and went on to describe how every day, when Saffron was small and lived downstairs in the green shuttered house where she, Antonia, lived upstairs, Saffron had run outside to talk to her angel. And from the petals of the yellow rose that grew up the garden wall ('See the rose!' said Antonia, interrupting herself to spin Sarah around to look at the old climbing rose tumbling down the wall behind her), Saffron had made for her angel yellow hats and shoes.

'Yellow hats and yellow shoes!' said Antonia, rubbing tears from her eyes, and then she had to pause to embrace Saffron all over again, and be surprised all over again, and Saffy had to gather some fallen petals from the yellow rose and sniff their faint sweet smell. When Antonia saw her do that she rushed to pick roses for her, laughing and flapping her hands at the thorns, and handing them eagerly to Saffron one by one. 'Hold carefully!' she said, as she passed over each flower. 'Hold very carefully!'

'But what *happened* to Saffy's angel?' asked Sarah a little bit impatiently, because the thing that had struck her first and most forcefully about this whole perfect little dream Italian garden was that it contained no angel. No angel anywhere. And that was what they had come for. Not roses.

Saffron's hands were full of roses.

'Saffy's angel?' repeated Sarah, persisting in sticking to the point, no matter how many roses barred the way. 'Saffy's angel?'

'Not Saffy's angel in those days,' said Antonia, passing Sarah a rose for herself ('Hold very carefully!'). 'My angel then! A long time ago, and so sad. You know how it was with Saffron's mother?'

Sarah nodded.

'Terrible. And so Saffron went to England with her grandpapa. You know?'

Sarah nodded again.

'So the angel also went to England!'

'What!'

'With Saffron's grandpapa. He took my angel away. One week only after he left with Saffron, and I thought I would not see either again, he came back. To buy my angel for Saffron. I would have given, but he said, no, he must buy!'

'Oh, Saffy!' breathed Sarah.

'Then off again to England, and I know this time I will not see him again. Write, I told him. Tell me about Saffron. He never wrote.'

Somehow Saffron seemed to have dropped her roses. Now she was on her knees, gathering them together again.

'He was ill,' she said, looking up at Antonia. 'He couldn't. He was ill for a long time before he died . . .'

'He has died? Your grandpapa?'

'Yes.'

'Oh no.'

'No one even knew he came back here. To Siena. They only knew he had a car crash. I suppose it must have happened on his way home.'

'Not another car crash?'

'Yes. And after it he didn't talk. He didn't talk to anyone, ever, for years and years and years.'

'Oh no.'

'Once he said "Saffron". "Saffron". That was all.'

'Super Hero,' said Sarah, a long time later, back in the little square. 'Are you all right?'

'Yes,' said Saffron. 'Yes, thanks, Mission Control. I am all right now.'

Then it was time to go home, and Saffron was still all right. Happy even. How strange it was, she thought, to have come so far, and found so little, and feel so contented. She did not understand it at all.

'Worth coming,' said Sarah's father cheerfully, driving across Italy very fast on the wrong side of the road. 'If only to get that fountain in the square fixed. What's the matter with those girls in the back? Take nothing seriously! That fountain was potentially lethal! One good hard frost and there would have been a sheet of ice all over the square! All right! All right! You laugh! Who wants to see me overtake a Ferrari?'

'NO!' said Sarah's mother.

'Too late! Look at that! He never knew what passed him! I've told the hotel manager we'll be back next year, Liz. Edward. That's his name.'

'Eduardo,' contradicted Sarah's mother.

'So he told me. "Edward", I said to him. "That's your name then." Very nice bloke. Showed me his office system. Absolutely up to date! Couldn't fault it.'

'Oh good,' said Sarah's mother sarcastically.

'Tried to be kind about English football. "Spare me!" I said. "A washout!" What's the Italian for a washout?'

'I haven't the faintest idea.'

'Couldn't find it in that phrase book. Not that it mattered. He understood. So anyway, I said we'd be back next spring. All right, Saffy? You on for another trip under the bean bag?'

'Yes please.'

'See your nice old lady again.'

'I said I'd write to her.'

'Good gracious, Saffy!' exclaimed Sarah's father, genuinely shocked. 'What's the matter with e-mail? How can I drive if everyone's giggling? Of course she'll be online. It's a mistake to treat people as if they're out of the ark, just because they're foreign. You've got to e-mail Edward when we get home, Liz. Promised you would.'

'Why?' asked Sarah's mother, suspiciously.

'Said you'd send some English recipes over for the kitchen. Fish pie. Yorkshire puddings. That sort of thing. Can't imagine what you girls find so funny. Make yourselves useful and look behind! That Ferrari's creeping back up on us!'

'Ignore him!' said Sarah's mother. 'He probably never even noticed you! Anyway, I think he's very silly, going so fast.'

'Really, Liz, you do talk some rubbish! Best drivers in the world, Italians! Everyone knows that! Watch his face when I put my foot down! When did you tell your folks you'd be home, Saffy?'

'Sunday morning,' said Saffron.

'Saturday night at this rate,' said Sarah's father happily.

Before they had left Siena Mrs Warbeck told Saffron to telephone the Banana House, just to let her family know they were starting for home. Saffron had done this, and as usual the call had been answered by Rose. Also as usual nobody else had been given a chance to speak and the news had to be dragged from Rose, bit by bit, by Caddy and Indigo.

'Did she sound happy?'

'No.'

'Oh Rose!'

'She sounded like she'd just been crying. And she didn't find her angel. It's gone. Grandad took it.'

'Rose! Did she tell you that? How do you know? You should have let someone else talk to her.'

'I can talk,' said Rose with dignity, levering open the lid of a large tin of brick red paint and looking speculatively inside. 'Look at this! I thought it'd do to brighten up my camels. I got it out of a skip.'

'Rose darling, tell us about Saffy.'

Rose poked a finger into her paint, lifted it out, and watched the silky drips fall with mesmerising slowness back into the can.

Caddy tried a different approach.

'You shouldn't take things out of skips.'

'Have to,' said Rose.

'But it *is* a perfect red for the camels.'

'Grandad took Saffy's angel,' said Rose, now stirring the paint with her finger as she spoke. 'He went back to Siena and fetched it for her. He brought it to England. Saffy said. Years ago, before I was born. So.'

'Saffy told you Grandad brought her angel back to England?' asked Indigo. 'Then what did he do with it?'

'Lost it,' said Rose. 'Saffy said. When he crashed his car probably. On his way home. Saffy says it doesn't matter any more. She'd been crying, though. I could tell.'

'Don't eat paint, Rose darling. Especially red. Poor Saffy.'

'But *I* thought,' continued Rose, only tasting a tiny bit of red, 'it wouldn't just disappear. And all Grandad's stuff is here. And Saffy's not back till Sunday so we've got ages to find it for her.'

'Here?' asked Indigo and Caddy, astonished.

'Course.'

'You think Saffy's angel is here? In this house?'

'Mmmm,' said Rose, fitting the lid back on to the

154

paint tin and whacking it down hard with her fist. 'All we have to do is find it.'

They were interrupted at that moment by a loud banging on the door. Caddy opened it and there was Michael on the doorstep, looking very impatient.

'Michael darling!' exclaimed Caddy.

'I hooted,' said Michael. 'I've been sitting there hooting for the last ten minutes. Are you ready?'

Often and often in Caddy's daydreams, Michael had appeared on the Banana House doorstep, asking impatiently 'Are you ready?' Caddy had been prepared for this moment for months.

'Absolutely,' she said at once, beaming happily at him. 'What for?'

'Driving test.'

Caddy stopped beaming.

'You forgot,' said Michael in disbelief.

Caddy nodded limply.

Michael began to beat his head against the doorframe.

'She's been working very hard,' said Indigo, appearing beside Caddy. 'Chemistry, Physics, Biology. All sorts.'

'Anyway,' said Rose, pushing in beside Indigo, 'she'd never have passed.'

'Yes,' agreed Caddy, beginning to edge gently away from the door. 'I think I shall have to cancel it, Michael darling. Because my mother is very busy painting in the shed and I have to look after Indigo and Rose. And hunt for Saffy's angel. And all these exams . . .'

Michael stopped beating his head, grabbed Caddy firmly by the elbow, marched her down the steps, opened the car door and pushed her into the driving seat. Indigo and Rose had one glimpse of her horrified face as she turned to look back at them and then there was a terrific roaring as Caddy started the engine in her usual frightening fashion. An assortment of lights flashed, the horn sounded, the car seemed to jump in the air like a cat, all four wheels off the ground together, and then Caddy and Michael were gone, leaving a patch of silence in the road where they had been.

'Oh well,' said Rose.

'Yes,' agreed Indigo, and added, to comfort himself more than anything, 'he's got an emergency brake on his side. He can stop her if he has to.'

'Let's find Saffy's angel before they get back. Where shall we start looking?'

'There's a lot of Grandad's stuff under my bed.'

'Come on then,' said Rose.

The Banana House had always had a slightly magical feel about it and this was because it was one of those places that appear to be bigger on the inside than they do on the outside. It seemed this way because of the amount of things it contained, far more than it was possible to imagine fitting into a house of even twice its size.

The contents of the Banana House were divided into three distinct levels, like geological ages.

The top level was made up of the stuff that was used every day. This included everything belonging to Rose, Indigo's Antarctic books, Caddy's hamsters, Saffron's hairbrush, nothing of Eve's, and a variable mixture of saucepans, paintbrushes, magazines and potted plants. Whenever tidying up was carried out it was this top layer that was tidied.

Beneath the top layer was a second, deeper one. Nearly everything belonging to Eve was there, along with a great many other things belonging to everyone else (except Rose). Sometimes from this depth forgotten objects would rise spontaneously to the surface, where they would be welcomed with cries of astonishment.

The third and deepest level was almost impenetrable except by using enormous effort. It was mostly made up of very heavy boxes and bulging bags.

It was this level that Rose and Indigo started to excavate in their search for Saffy's angel. They began under Indigo's bed.

'Nothing,' said Rose.

That was not exactly true. There had been eleven boxes of books under Indigo's bed, a roll of old carpet and the stuffed panda everyone supposed had been lost in the park eight years before.

Indigo and Rose left it all where it was and began on the two old suitcases that had been on the top of the wardrobe for so long they had almost become wardrobe-coloured. After the suitcases they went to the pile of boxes in the corner, and then they dragged everything out from under the chest of drawers.

'Nothing,' said Indigo, straightening up at last and rubbing his knees.

'Where next?' asked Rose.

'Bathroom,' said Indigo, and had soon moved the bathroom chair and the linen basket and become deep in the contents of the little box-like cupboard under the hot water tank.

'Nothing,' said Rose a few minutes later.

'Never mind,' said Indigo, who was beginning to enjoy himself very much. 'We've only just started.'

'We've blocked ourselves in,' observed Rose, looking at the pile of stuff between themselves and the bathroom door.

'Shove it in the bath!'

Hurriedly they piled everything they had discovered (an alternative set of Christmas decorations, Rose's old potty, seven hot water bottles and a lot of shoes) into the bath, and cleared a way on to the landing.

'Where next?' asked Indigo.

'Airing cupboard,' said Rose. 'Then those boxes in the corner. Then the other bedrooms, one by one.'

'As long as we don't muddle up Caddy's exam notes.'

'We won't,' said Rose.

The tremendous search went on and on, and the longer it lasted, the more gripping it became. Nothing so strenuous, so bold or so ruthless had ever before been attempted in the history of the Banana House. Together Indigo and Rose probed the darknesses of forgotten cupboards. Together they climbed on boxes balanced on boxes balanced on wobbling chairs and investigated the tops of high furniture. In their parents' bedroom they opened ancient trunks that had been closed for years and years.

Their arms ached and their eyes smarted with dust. They banged their heads and trapped their fingers and broke their nails. They stopped being surprised at anything they found. They almost stopped speaking to each other. Anyone listening from outside would have heard no more than thuds and dragging sounds, the occasional gasp of pain, and a few murmured words:

'There's another, further back.'

'Pull.'

'Got it.'

'Nothing.'

Sometime late in the afternoon Caddy came home, buried her head in a pile of chemistry notes, and burst into tears. Nobody heard her.

Later still Eve wandered in from her shed in a daze of Art. She put her arms round Caddy and sat rocking her saying, 'Darling, darling. There, there. Darling, darling,' until Caddy stopped sniffing and allowed her mother to bathe her face with cold water and a painty towel.

'There!' said Eve, when Caddy was better again. 'There, darling! Sit still and I will cook supper!'

Caddy sat still while Eve began peeling an enormous saucepanful of potatoes, frying sausages and onions together in a cloud of blue smoke, and opening tins of peas. This was an astonishing effort on Eve's part, and Caddy was very touched, especially when Eve began preparing the favourite pudding of her childhood, bananas split lengthwise and stuffed with chocolate, before being baked in their jackets in the oven.

Indigo and Rose, filthy and ravenous, came sniffing into the kitchen as soon as the smell of cooking drifted up the stairs. They noticed Caddy's red eyes, but kindly did not mention them, and ate their unexpected supper almost silently, still in a daze of adventure.

'What have you been doing?' Eve asked Rose.

'Finding things,' said Rose vaguely.

'What sort of things?'

'Nothing.'

'Saffron will be back on Sunday morning,' said Eve, feeling like a proper old-fashioned mother as she stacked up the sausage plates and began to hand out baked bananas, 'and Daddy's coming tomorrow . . . I wonder what we ought to tell him about Saffy going to Italy so unexpectedly . . . Stowing away. Not what Daddy would call a good idea.'

'Don't let's get Saffy in trouble,' pleaded Caddy. 'Just say she rushed off at the very last minute.'

'He won't like that either,' said Eve, worriedly. 'He likes things done properly. Planned. And talked over.'

'Say nothing,' suggested Indigo.

'But he'll wonder where she is on Saturday night.'

'Say she's with Sarah,' said Rose, 'and will be back in the morning. That's true. She will.'

'Do you really think that would be best?' asked Eve doubtfully.

'Oh yes,' said Rose.

Her mother still looked bothered.

'Darling Daddy,' said Rose cunningly.

This made up Eve's mind for her completely, and she said 'Clever Rose!', handed Caddy the last banana, smoothed a cobweb out of Indigo's hair, and left to spend the evening in her shed with an unusually free conscience.

'Come on!' said Indigo, as soon as the door had closed behind her. 'Saffy's angel!'

'Have you been looking all afternoon?' asked Caddy.

'Yes,' said Indigo. 'Nothing so far. But there's still all of downstairs. You can help.'

They began at once with the tops of the kitchen cupboards. Then there was the cupboard under the stairs which had been filled up years before and never opened since. Followed by the living room dresser (inside and underneath), the coal hole and the space behind the sofa. They found canvases and books and boxes of photographs, an old typewriter, another set of

Christmas decorations, bundles of curtains, a sewing machine, bags of clothes, a violin in a case, Caddy's dolls house, a baby carrier full of baby clothes, a tin of shells, flower pots, a cat basket and Eve's wedding dress.

Then finally there was nowhere else to look.

Chapter Twelve

It was Saturday morning. Eve had spent the night in her shed, as she often did, alternately painting and dozing and trying to make up her mind to go back to the house and go to bed properly. Caddy and Indigo and Rose, dropping with tiredness and disappointment, had struggled up the stairs, clambered over the great number of obstacles between themselves and their bedrooms, and collapsed, fully dressed, into immediate sleep.

Indigo slept, but his unconscious mind did not. All night it searched, as Indigo had searched, to find Saffy's angel. It ransacked his memories as Indigo had ransacked the house, and at the end of the search it woke him up.

Indigo sat up in bed and he was utterly astonished. He knew suddenly and as certainly as if he had seen it there himself, where Saffy's angel was.

Rose woke up, bounced from her bed, looked out of the window, and saw, with great surprise, that Michael's car was parked outside.

'I know, I know,' groaned Caddy sleepily, when

163

Rose tried to force her to get up to see for herself. 'It's been there all night.'

'Crashed?' asked Rose.

'Of course not crashed!'

'But where is Michael?'

'Gone off to Spain with Droopy Di,' said Caddy miserably.

'How do you know?'

'He told me he was going. And she collected him. On her motorbike, when he got back here. At least, I think it must have been her. Long gold hair.'

'What?'

'Long gold hair trailing down from her crash helmet. And incredible legs. And black leathers . . .' Caddy paused to blow her nose and wipe her eyes. '. . . I don't suppose I shall ever see him again. Or not after he's collected his beastly car! I'm not driving it!'

'What happened, Caddy?'

'I don't know! I don't know what went wrong. I'd worked out a plan to make sure I'd fail. I reversed up a kerb and the rotten examiner let me off . . .'

'Caddy,' asked Rose, light dawning at last. 'Did you pass your driving test?'

Caddy nodded, her face buried in her pillow, her shoulders hunched.

'We were sure you'd failed,' said Rose. 'That's why we never said anything yesterday. Now you won't have any more driving lessons.'

'No.'

'And no more Michael?'

'No.'

'But he said "Caddy darling" that time you told us about.'

'Yes, well, he's gone to Spain with Droopy Di.'

'The rotten pig!' said Rose.

She and Indigo met at the bathroom door, both bursting with news.

Indigo won.

He said, 'I've found Saffy's angel!'

'What?'

'At least, I've found where it is. It's in Wales. I've worked it all out. Caddy's house is in Wales. My car's in Wales. Saffy's angel's in Wales. Obviously.'

Rose's mouth fell open. She jerked it shut again.

'Wales,' said Indigo. 'That's where we need to look.'

'Michael,' said Rose, 'has gone to Spain with Droopy Di. And he's left Caddy his car to practise in. She wasn't crying because she failed her driving test, she was crying because of no more Michael. She's passed her driving test. So.'

Indigo felt suddenly ill. He felt like a stone falling from a precipice. He felt like a light blown out. He felt like a lump of ice dissolving into water. He fumbled for his voice and croaked, 'So what?'

Rose was not even there to answer. She was back in her bedroom relating Indigo's amazing new idea. Indigo could hear her.

'Quick Caddy! Let's go straight away! Before Saffy gets home, and before Dad turns up and stops us!'

'Go away, Rose darling, please!'

'Indigo might be right. Please let's go and look.'

'Another day.'

'There isn't another day. Come on, Caddy!'

'I don't know the way.'

'Indigo is fantastic at maps. Come on Caddy, you're a brilliant driver!'

'You know that's not true.'

'Indigo!' called Rose. 'Indigo, isn't Caddy a brilliant driver?'

'Ah . . . er . . . er . . .'

'See, Caddy!'

'I can't. Sorry Rose. I can't.'

'Why not?'

'Much too terrifying!'

'You're not scared!'

'Of course I am! Anybody would be.'

'I wouldn't be,' said Rose. 'Nor would Indigo, would you, Indigo?'

'Yes,' said Indigo.

'He means No,' said Rose. 'I know, Caddy! Just drive a bit of the way!'

'What?'

'A tiny bit. And then if you feel all right, a tiny bit more. And a bit more if you want to. And go back if you don't.'

'I can only drive slowly.'

'That's all right.'

'And I can only do left turns.'

Rose ran downstairs, grabbed a road atlas and ran

triumphantly back up again. 'Wales is left! Look! It's left all the way! So will you, Caddy? Try just a bit of the way? Going slow.'

'Oh Rose!'

Indigo knew then that she had given in, and that he would have to go with them and find the way by left turns all the way to Wales because that was where Saffy's angel was. He was terribly frightened.

Caddy, remembering her mother's distress when Saffron had stowed away to Italy, said, 'I'm not going anywhere without telling Mum,' and went out to the shed.

A faint hope had come to her that her mother might say she must not go. It was ridiculous really, Caddy knew. As far as she could remember, it had never happened before. Eve had, as far as possible, always let them do exactly as they liked. Sometimes she found it quite difficult to let them do *exactly* as they liked, when Indigo, for instance, took to climbing out of his bedroom window, or Rose deliberately wound her father up to fuming pitch, or Saffron ran away to Italy, or Caddy devoted her life to guinea pig breeding, as she had done two years earlier, and failed all her school exams. However, Eve always stuck out these grim times as bravely as she could. After all, she would tell herself, she had known from the day the children were born that they were in every way more talented, intelligent and wise than she would ever be. Remembering this was always a great

167

comfort to Eve. She thought they probably took after their father.

She was already at work when Caddy found her, surrounded by a muddle of Young Offenders art. Rose, who had followed after Caddy, at once bent down and began to examine it very critically.

'Terrible!' she said.

'Rose, darling!' protested her mother.

'Birthday card pictures, that's what they look like! Why are they here?'

'We're having an exhibition,' explained her mother. 'In the library. I'm hanging them this morning. I'm in an awful rush! Are you better, Caddy darling?'

'Yes thank you.'

'Lovely supper,' said Eve. 'Horrible Brain Juice for breakfast though. Don't tell Daddy.'

Brain Juice was a recipe invented by Eve years before, when she had had to stay awake all day to look after Caddy and Indigo and Saffron, and all night to take care of the fragile and impermanent baby Rose. It was Coca-Cola with a great deal of instant coffee stirred into it. It was black and frothy and gritty and it tasted like a primitive mediaeval poison, but it banished sleep like magic. The children's father disapproved very much of their mother drinking Brain Juice. Bill explained to her many times (from the peace of his London flat) how destructive to brain cells it was sure to be, but she did not seem to care.

'Can't think how people manage without it,' she said to Caddy and Rose, taking a huge, shuddering gulp. 'Shall you be all right today, while I'm hanging my Young Offenders?'

Caddy said she did not know, Rose and Indigo wanted her to drive them to Wales.

Eve went very still for a moment, remembering Caddy's tears after her driving test. Then she pulled herself together and said, 'Lovely, lovely! Pass me that little one of the cat with the flowers, Rose. Isn't it pretty?'

Rose said it was yuk.

'To find Grandad's old house,' said Caddy, 'to look for Saffy's angel.'

Rose distracted her mother just then. She found a handy paintbrush and a palette of oils and began touching up a Young Offenders portrait of Eve.

'Don't, Rose!' said Eve, distractedly, draining her glass of Brain Juice and immediately (with shaking hands) mixing herself another.

'But he's made your eyebrows meet in the middle!'

'Perhaps they do, to him,' said Eve. 'Tell me again what you just said, Caddy darling.'

'To look for Saffy's angel. I passed my driving test yesterday.'

Eve nearly fainted with relief.

'Caddy, how brilliant! First time too! It took me eleven tries! You are clever . . . Rose!'

'Can't I just uncross your eyes?'

'No, you really mustn't!'

'Michael has lent me his car, you see,' Caddy continued.

'Why do they sign their names so big?' asked Rose. 'Can't they write small?'

'Please put that down, Rose!'

'Fancy being called Brain!'

'Brian! He's called Brian.'

'He's spelled it wrong then. He's put Brain.'

'He can't have!' exclaimed her mother, grabbing it. 'Oh, the silly boy! Now I shall have to go all the way to the unit to get him to put it right! Caddy, darling, you will drive carefully, where ever you go? Because I know you've had nearly a hundred lessons and passed your test first time . . .'

'I've done it for you!' said Rose proudly, holding up the portrait, which now read:

Briain Sargent ~~Esq~~.

'I've crossed out the wrong bits,' said Rose smugly. 'And I've altered your teeth. No one has that many.'

Eve grabbed the picture, took a terrible swig of turpentine and choked. 'Never, *ever* drink turpentine, darlings!' she said, when she could speak again. 'It's frightfully bad for you,' she added, as she wiped her eyes and began frantically dabbing the picture with a rag dipped in Brain Juice. She counted quietly under her breath and when she got to thirty she managed to say, 'Have a lovely day, darlings!'

Eve always felt very sorry for mothers who hit their children. She thought they must feel dreadful afterwards.

★　★　★

Rose sat in the back. She had with her a large drawing pad and a box of bright felt-tips. She watched Indigo anxiously, afraid that his nerve would break before the journey had even begun. She need not have worried. Indigo had not spent so long training himself to deal with fear for nothing. He sat in the front beside Caddy, pale but certain. He had brought with him every map and atlas in the house, a box of tissues, and a blue plastic horror known to the family as the Sick Bowl.

'It's eighty miles,' he said. 'Show me the emergency brake.'

Caddy showed him and he practised pushing it in and out a few times.

'Are you sure you want to go?' Caddy asked him.

'Yes,' said Indigo. 'Because it's there. The more I think about it the more sure I am. And Saffy needs her angel.'

At first the journey seemed unreal. Caddy had driven the local roads and roundabouts so often with Michael that she almost forgot he was not beside her. Then gradually it all became less familiar.

Rose said in an interested voice, 'I've never been here before.'

This frightened Caddy. She panicked in the middle of a roundabout. The car stalled and would not start. Gradually it began rolling slowly back towards the car behind.

'Help, help!' squealed Caddy.

The car behind began to hoot. So did the lorry behind the car.

Rose coped with that. She grabbed her paper and a red pen and wrote in large letters and held the message up at the back windscreen.

BE NICE. DO NOT HOOT.

The hooting stopped.

Indigo stepped on the emergency brake and stopped the car rolling backwards. He began to speak just as Michael had spoken at the end of the awful driving lesson that had frightened him so much.

'Handbrake on,' said Indigo, and his voice even sounded like Michael's. 'Start the engine. Into first. Indicate.'

It might have been Michael, talking Caddy home, at the end of a stressful lesson.

Caddy said, 'Indigo darling!' and started the car, and they were on their way again.

Rose took down her message and wrote another one.

THANK YOU.

A stream of drivers overtook them, the ones who had hooted waving in a friendly fashion as they passed. Rose waved back and Indigo relaxed in his seat and Caddy began to sing. She sang a hymn she had learned at school when she was very little.

'When a knight won his spurs in the stories of old
He was gentle and brave (that's you, Indy!),
He was gallant and bold (that's you, Rose).'

There was another horrid moment when a dark shape on the road ahead resolved as they got closer, into all that was left of a run-over fox. Caddy swerved all over the road in her efforts to avoid it, tears rolling down her cheeks. The car behind swerved all over the road too, avoiding Caddy, and the driver shook his fist.

DON'T!

wrote Rose indignantly, and then, with Indigo's help, a whole series of messages:

THERE WAS A FOX
SQUASHED FLAT
POOR FOX
SHE IS CRYING
SO YOU HAD BETTER NOT
TRY PASSING US YET
I WILL TELL YOU WHEN IT IS SAFE

The driver of the car behind gave Rose a thumbs-up sign, to show he understood, and a few minutes later Indigo was able to stop passing Caddy tissues and they could write:

IT WILL BE ALL RIGHT NOW

'Everyone waves when they overtake,' observed Caddy innocently, knowing nothing of Rose's messages. 'I wonder why.'

'I make friends with them,' said Rose, busy writing again:

HELLO
WE ARE GOING TO WALES

Caddy craned her head round to see how Rose did it.

'Cadmium dear,' said Indigo at once and very reprovingly. 'Watch the road ahead!'

'Yes,' agreed Caddy sadly. 'That's how he talks. Darling Michael.'

'Don't call me darling,' said Indigo primly. 'I'm a driving instructor.'

Caddy began to giggle. 'I didn't know you could do people's voices!'

'Neither did I,' said Indigo.

'Do some more.'

'Keep checking your mirror,' said Indigo obligingly. 'It is either start passing exams, or a career as a small scale guinea pig farmer living at home with no transport. Think about that, Cadmium darling!'

Caddy had to pull over to laugh properly.

'How do you know he said that?'

'You told me,' Indigo reminded her.

'But how did you remember?'

'I always remember everything people say,' said Indigo, in his ordinary voice. 'Didn't you know I had photographic ears? We've done thirty something miles already.'

'Come on then,' said Caddy. 'Let's do a bit more.'

They drove on again until Rose announced from the back that she was starving.

'Me too,' said Indigo, realising with a sudden rush of joy that his sickness had disappeared miles before.

'I didn't bring any money,' said Caddy.

'I did,' said Indigo. 'I brought the housekeeping jar.

They stopped at a roadside van and bought bacon rolls and orange juice and had a very late breakfast in the morning sunshine. Indigo and Caddy bent over the road atlas and worked out a way of avoiding the next big town by detours down country roads.

'It will be a bit further,' said Indigo. 'But I don't think that will matter. It's not as if we're heading for the motorway.'

'No,' agreed Caddy solemnly. 'I don't think we are ready for the motorway yet.'

They drove on again.

'Fifty-five miles,' said Indigo. 'More than halfway. Much more.'

'Can't we go faster?' asked Rose.

'No!'

They made a new sign which Rose held up to the cars that came up behind them as they travelled along.

WE CAN'T GO FASTER

'We'll let them past at the next wide bit,' said Caddy.

WE'LL LET YOU PAST AT THE NEXT WIDE BIT

they wrote.

They stopped again for drinks and ice creams, and noticed how the countryside was becoming much hillier. They had not been back in the car for long when Indigo said suddenly, 'Wales!'

WELCOME TO WALES

read a sign at the side of the road.

WELCOME To WALES

wrote Rose triumphantly to the car behind.

Then there was a fast wide road and exciting glimpses of the sea on the right-hand side, and then a sign that might have been put up especially for them, the name of their grandfather's old village, six miles along, the next turn to the right.

It went very quiet in the car. It was so surprising to see it there.

Indigo and Rose wrote another sign:

WE ARE TURNING RIGHT
IN A MINUTE
SHE HATES TURNING RIGHT

The car that was following them obediently pulled back while Caddy accomplished this difficult manoeuvre.

'Can you remember the house?' asked Indigo.

'Yes,' said Caddy. 'I remember this road too. Sea all the way along one side. The house isn't really in the village. It's before you get there.'

A few minutes later Caddy stopped the car.

'It's that one,' she said.

★　　★　　★

Bill Casson had been nearly correct when he said that their grandfather's house was tumbling into the sea. It almost was. It was afternoon by now, and the sun was hot and bright, but even in the sunshine the house looked forlorn, its windows boarded up, its roof half open, barbed wire tangled round the gate and a notice:

DANGER
KEEP OUT

Several people had owned it since the Cassons' grandfather, holiday companies who had rented it out season after season until it was too dilapidated for even the most robust holidaymakers. However, to Caddy, Indigo and Rose it was still their grandfather's house.

'I wish we could see inside,' said Caddy, wistfully, but that was impossible. The doors were all locked and the windows tightly boarded over. They walked all round and then picked their way back through the thick, uncared for grass.

'I can't see any angels,' said Rose.

In the shattered garage at the end of the garden was the remains of their grandfather's Bentley, Indigo's car. The garage door was padlocked but they scrambled in through the empty window one by one to gaze at it.

'Fancy,' whispered Caddy.

The wheels were gone, and the windscreen was broken. The front was smashed. The seats were silted up with the dead leaves of all the autumns that had passed, blown in through the broken roof. It was no longer green, but grey with dust and cobwebs.

Indigo went round the back to the half open boot. It too, was full of rubbish and leaves.

'It's got to be here somewhere,' he said, scrabbling down among the dead leaves with his hands. 'If the house is here and the car is here . . .'

He bent down to look underneath, and then gave a shout. Pushed against the far wall of the garage, half covered in leaves, was a long wooden box. Indigo squeezed round and began to pull it out.

'It's heavy,' he said, panting. 'It's got something in it . . . There! And see, it has writing on it! Is that Italian?'

Caddy bent to look more closely. It was the address in Italy they had found in Eve's book.

16 Via S. Francesco, Siena

There was no way of opening the box just then, it was nailed tight shut.

'Still,' said Rose, who could hardly lift it, 'it doesn't matter. It's either Saffy's angel or something just as heavy. Gold perhaps.'

'It might be just a box of tools,' said Caddy. 'Car tools or something.'

'Who would nail their tools up tight in a box?' asked Rose scornfully.

They carted it back out to the car, stowed it gently into the boot, and set out on the long drive back.

★   ★   ★

Bill Casson was on his way home. He was looking forward to it very much. Sometimes, if he stayed away from the Banana House for long enough, it became the most desirable place in the world. Mysteriously, in his remembering mind, the rooms unmuddled themselves. Eve became organised and stopped painting pictures of mythical summers, and concentrated on improving her cooking instead. Caddy was still golden Caddy, but her dress sense improved and she became hamster and guinea pig free. Saffron was still his dear little Saffron, but she no longer had a nose stud and she smiled a lot more. And Indigo became interested in football and Rose in Barbie dolls.

This family of children so like, and yet so unlike, his own were so real in their father's head that he had actually bought a football and a Barbie doll and packed them up amongst his luggage to bring out as surprises.

So it was very disappointing for Bill to come home to find the Banana House in darkness and a note on the kitchen table saying his wife was hanging Young Offenders in the library and didn't know when she would be back.

Bill looked up from reading his note and gazed around the kitchen. Last night's disgusting, sausagey plates were stacked up unwashed in the sink. There were things all over the floor.

He went into the living room and there were things all over there too. Hundreds of things. Piles. The room looked ransacked.

179

Ransacked! thought Bill and turned and dashed up the stairs two steps at a time. There his fears were confirmed. Burgled. Ransacked and burgled.

It was too bad of Eve, thought her husband, to go and hang Young Offenders in the library and leave him to come home to a dark and burgled house.

He stumbled from room to room, trying to see what had been taken. Everywhere he fell over piles of things he did not know he owned. It occurred to him that it must have been an odd sort of burglar. The sort who brought things with them instead of taking them away. Boxes and boxes of things. Lorry loads.

There was a sound downstairs. The sort a burglar bringing in more rubbish might make. Bill leaped down to tackle him, and it was Eve.

Eve flung herself into his arms and wailed that she was so worried about darling Caddy.

'Caddy?' asked Bill, bewildered. 'What has Caddy done? Don't snuffle on my jacket, Eve darling!'

Caddy, explained Eve, snuffling on her sleeve instead, had passed her driving test only the day before, and set off for Wales today . . .

'*To Wales!*' repeated Bill.

'With Indigo and Rose . . .' continued Eve.

'*With Indigo and Rose!*'

'. . . To look for Saffy's angel . . .'

'*Saffy's angel?* None of this makes sense! Where is Saffy? Is she with the others? Is she here?'

Saffy was quite all right, Eve told Bill. She had run away to Siena with the wheelchair girl whose name was Sarah, and whose parents had been very kind.

'But . . .' said Bill, 'Saffy's all right, you say?'

'Yes, yes!'

'And the other three are gone off, heaven knows where?'

'They've been gone all day!' moaned Eve.

'And meanwhile we've had this burglary?'

Eve said what burglary, and when shown the state of the house said Oh, she thought that was just the children looking for something. Which brought them back to Caddy and Indigo and Rose again, and would have been very traumatic if they had not suddenly heard a tremendous hooting outside.

Eve and Bill hurried to the door in time to see Caddy and Indigo and Rose climb stiffly out of the car. Instead of rushing to the Banana House however, they turned and ran back up the road, where two people, one in a wheelchair, were hurrying to meet them.

'Saffy! Saffy!' cried Indigo.

'We've got it! We've got it!' shrieked Rose.

'Saffy darling!' exclaimed Caddy. 'Sarah darling! You're home!'

Sarah's father had been right and it had been Saturday night instead of Sunday morning when they got back, and Saffy and Sarah had dashed straight up the road to the Banana House.

'To surprise you,' said Sarah.

Bill said that he didn't understand anything that had happened.

'Since when?' asked Sarah politely.

Bill held his head in his hands and said he couldn't say since when. It probably went back years.

'Come indoors and we will tell you everything at once,' said Sarah kindly.

This turned out to be not possible. The talk went on all evening, and far into the night, and it was very nearly Sunday morning before the explanations were all over, and the lid of the box that Caddy and Indigo and Rose had brought back from Wales was finally lifted away.

Inside was Saffy's angel.

For Saffron, it said, in shaky old writing on the damaged base, and on the other side, *Saffy's angel*.

Saffron, picking up the broken fragments one by one said it didn't matter. She hugged Rose and Indigo and Caddy and Sarah, and said again and again that it didn't matter, it didn't matter at all.

Sarah's parents came to collect their daughter at midnight, and Sarah's mother said, 'Good night, Saffy, dear. I am so pleased you came with us! But I can see you are glad to be back!'

'How?' asked Sarah, and her mother said,

'Look how her eyes are shining!'

'No place like home, is there, Saffy?' asked Sarah's father, smiling down at her.

'No,' said Saffy, smiling back. 'No, there's no place like home.'

Epilogue in the Garden

Sometimes Saffron thought of her angel, and she could not help being a little sad, because after all the trouble everyone had taken to find it for her, it was broken. Still, there was too much going on at the Banana House for anyone to be sad very often. There was Permanent Rose, and her perpetual demands for more paint and bigger brushes. There was Indigo, now enrolled into the climbing club at the gym and being taught to abseil properly out of his bedroom window by Michael. Also there was Michael himself, who haunted the house on his weekends off, aggravating Bill very much.

'Hired him to teach m'daughter to drive,' said Bill to Eve, looking with disfavour at Michael's earring and the red elastic band that held up his ponytail. 'Didn't ask him to take over the family. He's got a nerve!'

Eve, who liked Michael, made soothing noises and took Bill to her shed to see her latest picture. It was an abstract painting, and it was called *Cadmium, Saffron, Indigo, Rose* and it was so good that Bill did not know what to say.

Sarah was also becoming one of the family. In fact she was so much a part of it that Eve had begun including her in her paintings. Bill did approve of Sarah and was always pleased to see her when she turned up on Sunday afternoons to help send him off to his other life in London.

A lovely man, thought Peter the taxi driver, watching in admiration the film star wave, and all the family enthusiastically waving back.

Soon, thought Saffron, on one of those Sundays, we shall be waving goodbye to Caddy as well.

Caddy had passed her exams at last and was going to university. She was leaving in the autumn, and already there had been a few frosty nights, and the first bright leaves were beginning to fall.

'They are Caddy's colours,' said Rose, gathering them up, and so they were, Cadmium Lemon, Cadmium Deep Yellow, Cadmium Scarlet and Cadmium Gold.

The nights were cold now, but the sunshine in the daytime was lovely. On the day before Caddy was to go away, Rose and Indigo, Sarah, Saffron and Michael were all outside, sprawled on the lumpy lawn of the Banana House, waiting for her to join them.

'What *is* she doing?' asked Michael impatiently.

'She's fetching something,' said Indigo. 'A surprise.' He looked carefully away from Saffron as he spoke, because he had been in on the secret, and knew what the surprise was to be.

'Can't wait for ever,' grumbled Michael.

'Why not?' asked Rose, sternly. 'Why can't you wait

for ever? You might have to when Caddy gets to university. I bet she has thousands of boyfriends.'

'Queuing up,' agreed Saffron. 'All round London.'

'Better get used to waiting,' advised Sarah.

Michael groaned and buried his face in the fur of a passing guinea pig.

'It's all your fault,' Saffron told him. 'Yours, and that Droopy Di's. You started Caddy off passing all those exams. So it serves you right.'

'Let's just blame Droopy Di,' said Michael, 'because of my broken heart.'

'Anyway,' said Rose. 'You've still got *her.*'

'Who?'

'Droopy Di, of course.'

'Oh yes,' said Michael. 'She will be a great comfort.'

'You made her up, didn't you?'

'Hmmm.'

'Didn't you? Who was it who collected you and took you off to Spain. It wasn't Droopy Di was it?'

'Hmmm.'

'Tell me,' said Rose, attacking him.

'All right. It was just a friend. There never was a Droopy Di. Don't tell Caddy!'

'I wonder what will happen to Michael when Caddy goes to London,' remarked Sarah to no one in particular.

'He will be blotted out of existence,' said Michael sadly. 'Along with the hamsters and the guinea pigs.'

'Indigo's looking after them,' said Rose. 'He hates furry animals. They are his next big challenge.'

'And who is looking after you and Indigo?' enquired Michael. 'Sorting out your party dresses and faking your paintings and talking you down from windowsills?'

'Me and Saffy, of course,' said Sarah. 'And do cheer up a bit, Michael! In only three and a half years' time I will be old enough to learn to drive. Think of that!'

'She likes to go fast,' said Indigo, glancing fondly across at Sarah, the latest member of his pack. 'Very fast, on the wrong side of the road, Saffy says.'

'Oh great,' said Michael. 'I'll look forward to that.'

'Caddy's coming now,' said Indigo, who was watching the house.

Caddy came out of the door as he spoke. She was carrying a box. It was the one that had held the fragments of the stone angel. Caddy had spent weeks over it. She had found the right kind of resin and one by one she had set the fragments together again, strapping each piece until it was solid, before adding the next. Then she had rubbed down each careful join with the finest grade of sandpaper. Last of all she had blown on to it a very little thin gold dust, Siena coloured. She had been able to find exactly the right shade from the ever-useful paint chart on the kitchen wall.

Caddy put the box down on the grass and took off the lid. Inside was the little stone figure that had come so far. Caddy lifted it out, and stood it carefully in the sunshine.

'Look!' she said. 'Look at Saffy's angel!'

GUILDFORD **college**

Learning Resource Centre

Please return on or before the last date shown.
No further issues or renewals if any items are overdue.

Class: ___EF MCK___

Title: ___Saffy's Angel___

Author: ___McKay, Hilary___